Monarchs *of the* Nile

By the same author:

Egyptian Rock-cut Tombs (1991)

The Canopic Equipment of the Kings of Egypt (1994)

After the Pyramids (2000)

*The Coffins and Canopic Equipment from
the Tomb of Tutankhamun* (in preparation)

With Salima Ikram:

Royal Mummies in the Egyptian Museum (1997).

The Mummy in Ancient Egypt (1998)

The Ancient Egyptian Tomb (in preparation)

Monarchs
of the
Nile

Second Edition

Aidan Dodson

The American University in Cairo Press
Cairo • New York

The American University in Cairo Press

First published in Egypt in 2000 by
The American University in Cairo Press
113 Sharia Kasr el Aini
Cairo, Egypt
http://aucpress.com

First published by the Rubicon Press 1995
Second, revised edition 2000

Dar el Kutub No. 9219/00
ISBN 977 424 600 4

Printed in Egypt

*To the memory of Professor A.F. Shore (1924-1994),
Brunner Professor of Egyptology at the University of
Liverpool, 1974-1991*

Contents

List of Illustrations

14. The pyramid of King Sahure at Abusir: view up the causeway to the entrance of the mortuary temple.

15. Harkhuf and his son; on one African expedition, he obtained a dancing *deneg* that delighted his child-king, Pepy II; tomb A.8 at Aswan, Qubbet el-Hawa (from Maspero, *Dawn*, 433).

16. Kings Inyotef I, II & III, from a memorial erected by Montjuhotpe II in the temple at Tod (Cairo Museum JE 66331).

17. The painted sandstone statue of King Montjuhotpe II, from his jubilee cenotaph at Deir el-Bahari (Cairo Museum JE 36195).

18. King Montjuhotpe II, embraced by Re; from the rear part of his temple at Deir el-Bahari (British Museum EA 1397).

19. King Sesostris III: a granite statue from the temple of Montjuhotpe II at Deir el-Bahari (British Museum EA 684).

20. The 'Fish-offerers' double statue of Sesostris III and Ammenemes III; from Tanis (Cairo Museum JE 18221 = CG 392).

21. King Ammenemes III, from Hawara (Cairo Museum CG 385).

22. The head of the mummy of King Taa II, showing the horrific wounds that caused his death (Cairo Museum CG 61051; from G.E. Smith, *The Royal Mummies* [Cairo, 1912], pl. ii).

23. The co-rulers, Hatshepsut and Tuthmosis III, depicted on the Red Chapel, a quartzite shrine erected by the queen at Karnak.

24. The mortuary temple Hatshepsut at Deir el-Bahari.

25. Hatshepsut's obelisks, from her Karnak Red Chapel (formerly Luxor Museum J.138).

26. King Tuthmosis III smites his enemies (south face of the Seventh Pylon at Karnak).

27. Quartzite head of King Amenophis III, from his mortuary temple at Thebes; this fragment once formed part of a standing figure, over 8 metres tall (British Museum EA 6).

28. Three commemorative scarabs of the reign of Amenophis III: 'Lake', 'Marriage' and 'Lion Hunt' examples (Museum of Fine Arts, Boston, 1972.873, 1985.420 and 04.1810).

29. Glazed steatite statuette of Queen Tiye (Louvre Museum E 25493 + N 2312).

30. The Colossi of Memnon, the quartzite statues of Amenophis III that stood at the entrance of his now-vanished mortuary temple.

Acknowledgments

Most Egyptologists possess the intention to write 'their' history of Egypt at some stage in their career. This book could perhaps be viewed as the edited highlights of what may (or may not) one day grow into something larger: in any case, my thanks go to George Hart for his part in bringing about its appearance at this particular point in time, as well as Anthea Page and Juanita Homan for publishing its first edition, and Neil Hewison and Pauline Wickham for their part in this one.

Unless otherwise stated, all photographs were taken by the author, with acknowledgments to objects' owning institutions. My illustrative thanks also go to Jacke Phillips for allowing me to raid her Sudanese archive,

Salima Ikram stands in my debt for her role in the publication of this second edition, as well as standing amongst those of my friends and family to whom gratitude is owed for reading and commenting upon the manuscript of the first edition: the others are Don and Edna Dodson, Christine Everall, Nicole Mostafa (née Freeman), Julie Hudson, Linda Pike and Niamh Wall. I am especially indebted to Linda for the time and effort she took to excise obscurities and other more unfortunate 'Dodsonisms' from the very first drafts of the text; Julie also deserves particular thanks, for her painstakingly proof-reading of the penultimate draft of the first edition, in spite of the heavy burden of finishing off a book of her own to a tight schedule. Finally, I would like to thank my wife, Dyan Hilton, for all her help with with proof-reading the final draft of the manuscript of this edition, and for all her support. To one and all, however, I would like to wish 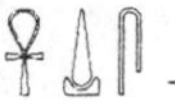 – 'Life, Prosperity and Health!'

Preface

The kings of Egypt have exerted a fascination in the West since time immemorial. Initially this was through their appearances in the Bible; more recently as a result of the nigh-on two centuries of excavation that have revealed to the world the physical remains of the kings, their people and their culture. The peak of popular interest was probably reached as a result of the 1922 discovery of the tomb of Tutankhamun, rekindled by the touring exhibition of some of that king's treasures in the 1960s and 1970s. Now, ancient Egypt is part of the curriculum of many schoolchildren, as well as having spawned large numbers of enthusiast-groups around the world, thus guaranteeing continuing awareness of the ancient civilization at all levels of society.

A considerable number of histories of ancient Egypt exist, but all of the more recent ones adopt a fairly broad-brush approach, in which the individual rulers are made to take fairly subsidiary roles in the general sweep of events. The only books to look at matters on a detailed king-by-king basis are far too out of date to bear any kind of use, and any new in-depth study along such lines is a long way off.

Against this background, the present volume attempts to present to a general audience concise accounts of the lives and times of some of the more significant – and/or interesting – occupants of the Egyptian throne, from the unification of the country around 3000 BC, down to the extinction of native rule just under three millennia later. It does not pretend to substitute for a proper history, but aims to provide something of a continuous narrative through the employment of fairly extensive summaries of prior/subsequent events as parts of the actual biographies.

Some of the rulers included, such as Tuthmosis III, had a major impact on their time, and were remembered by their own people until the very civilization collapsed. Others, such as Tutankhamun, were soon forgotten by the Egyptians themselves, only to burst into popular culture thousands of years after their deaths, as a result of the labours of modern archaeologists. Still more remain unknown outside the small circle of professional Egyptologists, but had careers that call out for wider dissemination. It has been my intention to provide a mix of all three categories, in an attempt to present a balanced view of Egyptian kings and their spectrum of achievements.

In doing so, one becomes painfully aware of the gaps in our knowledge, and the wide range of the possible interpretations that can be placed on a single body of 'hard' evidence. Indeed, on some subjects, such as the reigns of Akhenaten and his successors (the so-called 'Amarna Period' of the Eighteenth Dynasty, c.1390-1300 BC), there are probably as many reconstructions as there are Egyptologists who have considered the matter. In view of this, any attempt at presenting a fully 'balanced' account of certain pharaohs would involve disfiguring the narrative with so many digressions and summaries of the various arguments as to make it virtually unreadable. Accordingly, I have made the conscious decision to omit such matter as far as possible, restricting myself in all but a few cases to using the words 'probably', 'perhaps' and so-forth where problems exist.

The reconstructions given thus reflect what I believe to be the best or most likely readings of the available evidence, some of which has only emerged in the last year or two. Indeed, there are a number of cases where I have considerably revised my opinions, as compared with that expressed in the first edition of the book, and which may yet need further modification should it ever go to a third edition.

For those who wish to investigate matters further, and/or learn more about some of the alternate views held on various points, a *Guide to Further Reading* will lead the individual around the basic bibliography of each reign dealt with. Concerning this section, a conscious decision was taken to restrict entries almost exclusively to books in English, partly to keep its size down to manageable proportions, and partly with a view to the target readership of this volume and the kind of works that are likely to be available in, or through, public libraries. For those who desire to delve still deeper, most of the works cited contain extensive bibliographies, which will allow access to primary and secondary literature in periodicals and/or foreign languages.

As far as practicable, I have concentrated on the lives and acts of the kings and (ruling) queens themselves, with their monuments given secondary importance. For some monarchs, however, their monumental tombs represent *all* that is known of them, and there one has had to treat them in rather more detail than would be the case if rather more sources of information were available. This is particularly the case in the chapters covering the Archaic Period and Old Kingdom. Even then, an attempt is made to venture beyond bald description to allow the reader to gain some appreciation of the individuals who were *Monarchs of the Nile*.

Department of Archaeology   AIDAN DODSON
University of Bristol
1 March 2000

I   The Land and its People

The modern Arab Republic of Egypt (A.R.E.) occupies 992,000 square kilometres of the north-east corner of the African continent. However, only a tiny proportion – 4% – of the territory is inhabited. A small number of the population live in the oases of the Western Desert, but the overwhelming majority live in a narrow strip bordering the River Nile. Indeed, it is as this strip of land that Egypt has of old been defined, the two being so nearly synonymous.

This fertile band divides into two distinct elements. In the south, the cultivable area varies in width from nothing to a number of kilometres, beyond which it gives way to low desert that rapidly rises up to the arid plateaus of the Eastern (Arabian) and Western (Libyan) Deserts. In contrast, the Delta, beginning just north of modern Cairo, spreads out in a great triangle towards the Mediterranean, with kilometre upon kilometre of flat, fertile land, cris-crossed by canals and wholly dissimilar to the valley in both appearance and ethos.

Traditionally, the ancient Egyptian state was held to have extended from the shores of the Mediterranean to Aswan; however, at many points in its history, it reached far south into Nubia, encompassing the southern part of the A.R.E. and the northern part of the Democratic Republic of the Sudan. This section of the Nile, now lost below the waters of Lake Nasser, created by the building of the High Dam at Aswan, was far more barren than that further north, and mainly of interest as a source of raw materials and a trade-route to the far south. Communication south of Aswan was hindered by a series of cataracts, or rapids, the First just above that city, the Sixth and last just below modern Khartoum.

It has become the ultimate Egyptian cliche to describe Egypt as being the 'gift of the Nile', a phrase coined by the Greek writer

1

Hecetaeus, and almost universally mis-attributed to the famous traveller Herodotus, who visited Egypt around 450 B.C.. By this he meant that without the river, the country and its civilization would not – could not – have existed in anything like the form that is so well known. Outside the margins of the river and the handful of oases, the country is desert, incapable of supporting a sedentary population, and inhabited solely by nomads, whose modern representatives are the *bedouin*.

Today, agriculture in Egypt is predicated upon perennial irrigation, made possible by a series of dams built across the river since the beginning of the twentieth century. However, until this change in the river regime, the growing of crops depended on the annual, natural, inundation of the Nile. In summer, rains in the Ethiopian highlands swell the river's tributaries, the Atbara and Blue Nile; today, this merely restocks Lake Nasser, but in the past, it led to the flooding of the Nile valley and delta, an inundation given divine personification as Hapy. The water, covering all of the agricultural land, receded in October/November, leaving behind on the fields a rich layer of alluvium. In this, crops were planted, ready for the harvest in March/April, with little or no watering required in the interim.

So fundamental to the Egyptian way of life was this cycle that the three calendrical seasons were named *Akhet* (Inundation), *Peret* (Growing) and *Shemu* (Drought). Each was divided into four thirty-day months, added to which were five festival-days, together making up a civil year of 365 days. The lack of a leap-year, to take into account the 365¼-day solar year, meant that the calendar gradually slipped until the season-names bore no relation to the agricultural cycle; only after 1,460 years did the seasons and calendar slip back into synchronization..

Agriculture was the principal occupation of the Egyptian population, based upon small villages, dotted up and down the river. The nature of the inundation system meant that, apart from the period after the rising of the water, when dykes would have to be maintained to prevent the water from leaving the fields too early, or flooding habitations, and the physical sowing and harvesting of crops, work was rather easier than under perennial cultivation methods: on the other hand, it meant that men could more easily be diverted to labour on public works, as they frequently were. The fairly low ancient population in pharaonic times, no more than four or five million, additionally meant that agriculture did not need to be particularly intensive to provide for adequate sustenance, plus a surplus – particularly for the taxes which were needed to support the many activities of the State.

Land was worked by a wide variety of private individuals and state organizations. Prominent amongst the latter were the temples, which owned huge areas of arable and grazing land, together with livestock and the tied labour to work it. The produce went towards the offerings to the deity, paying his or her priests, and part-funding building and restoration costs, together with the wide variety of activities which focussed on a cult centre.

While the state cults – Amun of Thebes, Ptah of Memphis, Re of Heliopolis, and many more – had large full-time staffs, the far

Fig. 1. The Nile inundation at Dahshur: in the background are the ruined 'Black Pyramid' of Ammenemes III and the 'Bent Pyramid' of Seneferu.

3

more numerous local deities often had their shrines manned on a part-time basis, whereby local people of a certain standing spent a number of months of the year serving as their god's priesthood. Thus, a priest will frequently also have been a farmer, a scribe, a soldier or a craftsman: religion was just one of a person's civic duties, rather than a specific vocation.

This rather effectively characterises the all-pervading nature of ancient Egyptian religion: rather like Islam, it was bound up in a way of life, making it very difficult to separate out the sacred and the profane. Personal piety was far more concerned with a person's own relationship with his or her preferred god than the massive ceremonial that surrounded the state gods. Indeed, the latter was a wholly different facet of man's relationship with the divine sphere, being more part of the magical maintenance of the universe than the simple giving of praise and offering of prayers. Where the two aspects might coincide was in the area of oracles. On festival days, the cult-statue of the deity would be carried out of his or her temple in procession, and individuals might place petitions before the image, to which the god would indicate assent or rejection.

Local government was carried out by councils, the *kenbut*, comprising the more prominent individuals of the area, with functions both administrative and judicial. Throughout historic times, the country was divided into provinces (nomes), their numbers varying at different periods. At particular points in Egyptian history, they were key administrative units; at others, they seem to have been little more than nominal groupings of towns. The other important administrative division was between the Nile valley and its delta. At certain times, each half of the country might have a discrete body of officials; in periods of disorder, the two elements had a tendency to become independent polities.

The population of Egypt has always been mixed, varied racial types, ranging from the light skin-tones of the north to the dark brown seen in the far south. Negroid features are to be found in the areas of the ancient kingdom that penetrated deep into the modern Sudan. In addition to the indigenous population, the country was subject to considerable immigration, peaceful and warlike, particularly into the north-east Delta – as witnessed by the Bible stories of Abraham and Joseph. By later times, Egypt

4

was thus a fairly cosmopolitan society, with foreign gods worshipped in a number of centres, and men of foreign extraction holding senior government and military positions.

The position of women in Egyptian society seems generally to have been much higher than usual in ancient civilizations; although restricted in the range of occupations open to them, they appear to have been fully competent at law – i.e. without a need to be under the tutelage of a male – and in some instances, literate. While the known examples of female pharaohs are exceptional, that they were able to hold the throne at all bears witness to the status of women.

Based upon the prominence of the funerary monuments of the Egyptians, modern popular opinion generally holds the view that they were a gloomy folk, obsessed with death and the preparations for it. However, even the most superficial study of the available material gives the lie to this: it is quite clear that the Egyptian character was fully the opposite. Their funerary preparations were rather a manifestation of a desire to prolong earthly life into eternity: Heaven was seen quite simply as a bigger, better, Egypt. There can be few more satisfactory endorsements of a society than for its citizens to desire its indefinite continuity.

II   The Egyptian Monarchy

At the pinnacle of Egyptian society sat the king. Below him were the layers of the educated bureaucracy, comprising nobles, priests and civil servants, and under them the great mass of the people, largely living an agricultural life. Except in the earliest times, when the highest official seems to have been the Chancellor, for most of Egyptian history, the senior official was the Vizier (*tjaty*), roughly equating to a modern Prime Minister. In New Kingdom times, two vizierates existed, responsible for Upper and Lower Egypt respectively. Below the vizierate, other officials were responsible for the treasury, agriculture, and the numerous other ramifications of the state. All bore with pride the title 'scribe' (*sesh*): in a world where literacy was the rare exception, the ability to wield the pen was to have the potential to wield power.

The king himself was the figure upon whom the whole administrative structure of the state was predicated. He was the head of the civil administration, the supreme warlord, and the chief priest of every god in the kingdom: all offerings were made in his name, by a priesthood acting in his stead. In addition, he was himself a divine being, the physical offspring of a god. Accounts of a ruler's divine birth centre on the god assuming the form of (or becoming incarnate in) the king's father, who then impregnated his wife, who accordingly bore the divine ruler.

In many accounts, the king is viewed as an incarnation of Horus, a falcon god, the posthumous son of Osiris, a divine king slain by his brother, Seth. Horus fought his uncle for the return of the throne, and part of the accession process of a king was the proper burial of his predecessor, as Horus carrying out the last rites for Osiris. There are a number of cases whereby such an act may have been the legal basis for a commoner's ascent of the throne. More usual, however, was the succession of the eldest son, whose status as heir may have been proclaimed during his father's life-time. In a considerable number of cases this was taken a step further by the heir's coronation as *co-regent*, henceforth ruling as an equal partner with his father. A point which has led to much confusion is the fact that while the younger king sometimes only began to count his regnal years after the death of his sire, in others, he started to do so from the moment of his coronation, thus leading to two dating systems running in parallel. Since the Egyptians did not use 'era' dating (such as 'BC' and 'AD'), relying on regnal dating, the potential difficulties for modern (if not ancient) historians can easily be imagined.

There is no evidence whatsoever for the old idea that the right to the throne was carried by the female line, meaning that a putative king had to marry the daughter of his predecessor, even if she were his full-blooded sister. Brother-sister marriages *did* occur in the royal family, but with sufficient irregularity for the motivation to be sought elsewhere.

The title of 'pharaoh' has come to us from the Old Testament. It originates in the Egyptian *per-aa*, 'great house', a designation of the palace, which first came to be used as a label for the king around 1450 BC, and becomes common only some centuries later. For most of the time, the usual word for king is *nesu*, but a whole range of titles were applicable to any full statement of a king's names and titulary.

From around 2500 BC onwards, an Egyptian monarch had five names. The first was the Horus-name, written inside a frame surmounting a representation of the facade of a palace (*serekh*: ▥), the falcon of the god Horus, patron of the monarchy, perched atop it. The second, the *Nebty* ('Two Ladies')-name, linked the king with the patron goddesses of Upper and Lower Egypt, while the third was the *Bik-nub* ('Golden Falcon')-name, whose significance has been much debated. Apart from the Horus-name, which was the principal means of designating the king during the very first few centuries of Egyptian history, these names were far less used than the remaining two, one or other of which became the usual way to refer to a king in both formal and informal contexts.

Both were enclosed in what is today referred to as a *cartouche*, from the French for a gun-cartridge. Representing a double rope, encircling the dominions of the king, the oval enclosure

7

(▢) was called by the Egyptians *shenu*. The first of the names contained within a cartouche is today referred to as the *'prenomen'*, and was usually preceded by the titles *Nesu-bity* ('King of Upper and Lower Egypt', or perhaps 'Two-aspected King' – the point is currently under debate) or *Neb-tawy* ('Lo·.¹ of the Two Lands', referring to the valley and delta areas of Egypt). It was, like the preceding three names, composed on the king's accession, and almost invariably incorporates the name of the sun-god, Re.

The second cartouche-name, the *'nomen'*, was preceded by the titles *Si-Re* ('Son of Re') or *Neb-khau* ('Lord of Appearances', or possibly 'Crowns'). It usually represented the birth-name of the king, sometimes, particularly in later periods, with some form of additional epithet, such as 'beloved of Amun' (*mery-Amun*), or 'divine ruler of Thebes' (*netjer-heqa-Waset*). It is by their nomina that the ancient kings are referred to by modern historians, who distinguish like-named individuals by the addition of ordinals such as 'II' or 'VI'. In ancient times, kings of the same birth-name were distinguished by their distinctive prenomina, it being extremely rare to find precisely the same combination of cartouche names being used by different pharaohs.

Since the Ancient Egyptian scripts do not write vowels, vocalization of names presents some problems, although there are conventions that allow acceptable transcriptions to be made: for example, the king *'Imn-mss* is usually referred to as Amenmesse. However, for a number of kings, *Greek* transcriptions survive, and one convention, adopted in this book, is that where these are tolerably close to the Egyptian skeleton, they will be used. Thus, a King *Dḥwty-ms*, who might otherwise be transcribed 'Djhutmose' or 'Thutmose', becomes 'Tuthmosis', *S-n-Wsrt* ('Senusret'/ 'Senwosret') becomes 'Sesostris', *Hnmw-ḫw.f-wỉ* ('Khnum-khufu') becomes 'Kheops', and, at the extreme of the technique, *Nsỉ-b3-nb-ddt* ('Nesibanebdjed') becomes 'Smendes'

Many of these Greek writings derive from a history of Egypt written in that language around 300 BC by an Egyptian priest named Manetho; excerpts of it survive in the works of later antique authors. In its text, he divided up the royal succession into thirty 'dynasties', broadly corresponding to our royal 'houses' of Plantagenet, York, Windsor, &c. Although there are numerous problems with Manetho's system, it is retained by Egyptologists to this day as the most straightforward way of reckoning the progress of the ancient civilization.

These dynasties are usually grouped into 'periods' and 'kingdoms', corresponding to distinct phases in the country's political or cultural evolution. Thus, the Old Kingdom embraces the Third to Sixth Dynasties, the time occupied by the great pyramid builders, while the Middle Kingdom, comprising the later Eleventh, Twelfth and Thirteenth Dynasties represents a reunification of the country, consolidation and cultural development, and then decline. The New Kingdom (the Eighteenth to Twentieth Dynasties) is the era of Egypt's imperial power in Asia, seeing the construction of an empire that extended from the Sudan to the Euphrates. The three Intermediate Periods, following each of the 'Kingdoms', highlight centuries during which central authority was eroded, accompanied in some cases by foreign rule of parts of the country.

In addition to the Manethonic framework, we have a number of earlier, and thus far more reliable, king lists that help to confirm the ordering of rulers. These lists all date to the New Kingdom, and comprise an administrative listing, giving full reign lengths as well as royal names (the badly damaged Turin Canon), and four monumental offering lists, three of which place their contents in historical order. Of the latter, by far the best is that from the temple of Sethos I at Abydos; all of them, however, are incomplete and omit rulers for political and other reasons. However, the lists combine with contemporary monuments and documents to permit the construction of our modern framework of Egyptian history.

Putting absolute dates BC to the dynasties thus reconstructed is often difficult, and the subject of intense scholarly debate. Some astronomical events, recorded in monumental inscriptions and papyri, can be of some help, but all dates prior to 664 BC must be regarded as approximations only. Even in the New Kingdom, where dates are seemingly well established, reputable estimates can vary by up to fifty years; the further back one goes, the worse it gets.

The Egyptian monarchy lasted in a recognizable form for over three thousand years. Although many changes occurred during that time, almost all of the fundamentals remained in being. We may now move on to look in detail at the reigns of a number of the individuals that held the venerable office of pharaoh, beginning with the first of them all, and finishing with the last native Egyptian to do so. Even after he was driven from his throne, the monarchy was to remain in at least theoretical existence for further centuries until the primeval ways of life were driven out by the new tenets of Christianity and Islam.

III   The Founders

'Menes'

c. 3050-3000 BC

Human habitation of the area now labelled 'Egypt' goes back to Palaeolithic times, when the territory bore little resemblance to its form in the historic era, with what is now desert covered in forests, fed by numerous water-courses. Plentiful stone tools survive, particularly from the Middle Palaeolithic (*c.*100,000-50,000 BC) and later, referring to a hunting, fishing and gathering society.

The dawning of the Neolithic, with its adoption of agriculture, seems to have followed on from climatic changes around 7000 BC, producing what are referred to as the Fayoum A and B cultures in Lower Egypt. Separate material cultures flourished in Upper (i.e. southern) Egypt, the first known grouping being the Badarian, appearing just before 5000 BC. This then develops into the Naqada I (Amratian – *c.* 4000-3500 BC), Naqada II (Gerzean – *c.* 3500-3150 BC) and Naqada III (*c.* 3150-3000 BC) cultures, each distinguishable by their forms of pottery and other items. Collectively, they are known as the Predynastic Period.

By Naqada II times, it appears that various statelets were coming into existence up and down the Nile valley, with certain large and elaborate graves likely to be those of local chieftains. The most impressive of these is the decorated tomb 100 at Hierakonpolis (*c.* 3200 BC), its form heralding the shape of later royal tombs.

Naqada III ('Dynasty 0') witnessed the consolidation of these statelets into something approaching regional kingdoms, possibly under indirect influence from Mesopotamia, where a complex of city-states came into existence in the second half of the fourth millennium. A number of slate palettes, amongst the most

11

distinctive types of object of the period, depict military operations, and it is fairly clear that this formative period saw conflict between the incipient polities, leading to the creation of larger units, led by someone recognizable as a proto-pharaoh.

It would appear that just before 3000 BC, most of southern Egypt was under the control of one man. A number of these early kings are known, from the ancestral burial ground of Abydos and a number of inscribed pieces found at Hierakonpolis. Amongst the latter is a mace head of a ruler named 'Scorpion', who is depicted wearing the White Crown, the conical headdress that was always to be associated with Upper Egypt. At Abydos (Umm el-Qaab), cemetery U, excavated since 1988 by Günther Dreyer, included a large, elaborate tomb (U-j), which was quite possibly the last resting place of 'Scorpion'.

The greatest of the slate palettes, from Hierakonpolis and now in Cairo, appears to depict the last stage of the expansionistic conflicts between the regional kingdoms: the unification of the whole of Egypt under one ruler. On one side, the Horus Narmer is shown, wearing the White Crown, smiting an inhabitant of the marsh-country, presumably the Delta. On the other, he wears the Red Crown, traditionally that of Lower Egypt, preceded by standard-bearers, before whom lie ten headless bodies.

Although the usual reading of the palette is that it commemorates the actual Union of the Two Lands, the *sema-tawy* which was central to the conception of the pharaonic state, there are various uncertainties concerning this. In particular, there are doubts as to whether the Red Crown was really the primeval insignia of the north, or was assigned to it at a later date. However, whether the Horus Narmer was the physical unifier of Egypt or not, the union certainly occurred around his lifetime.

Later Egyptian tradition, from at least the New Kingdom onwards, attributed the unification to one 'Menes'. There has been much discussion as to which early king should be seen as the prototype of this heroic figure, the candidates being the Horus Narmer, his successor, the Horus Aha, or a conflation of them and perhaps other early monarchs, such as 'Scorpion'. In favour of a single character is an ivory label which may make 'Men' (Menes) the *Nebty* name of Aha – or just possibly his predecessor.

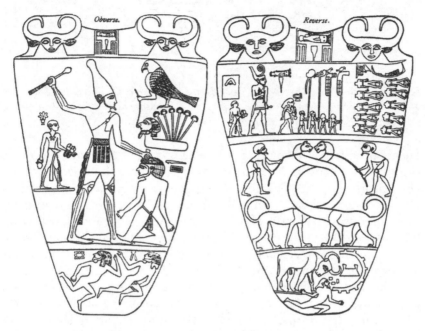

Fig. 2. The slate palette of the Horus Narmer, possibly recording the unification of Egypt; from Hierakonpolis. On the obverse, the king is shown wearing the crown of Upper Egypt, smiting an enemy who is identified as one of the 'Harpoon People'. The group above is a group of proto-hieroglyphs that relates to the capture of the people of the marsh-lands by Horus (=the king). These marsh-lands are presumably the Nile Delta. On the reverse, the Horus Narmer wears the Red Crown and, preceded by standard-bearers, views the decapitated bodies of his enemies, while at the bottom, as a bull, he demolishes an enemy stronghold.

The Horus Narmer seems to have married one Neithhotep, whom some have seen as a northern princess, cementing in her person the union of the country. She died during the reign of the

Fig. 3. Scenes from the Great Mace Head of the Horus Narmer. This has generally been interpreted as depicting the marriage of the king and Princess Neithhotep.

Horus Aha, her putative son, and was buried at Naqada, of old the centre of prehistoric Egyptian culture. Her tomb there is one of the earliest monumental buildings in Egypt, a brick *mastaba* (bench-shaped tomb) with its interior filled with store-rooms, and its exterior decorated with recessed panelling. This motif, which is ubiquitous during the Archaic Period, is common in Mesopotamia, and is one of the pieces of evidence cited for a connection between the two regions in this formative period.

Regardless of which of the contemporary kings should be seen as having been Menes, folk-tales, as recorded by the Greek historian, Herodotus, state that the king founded the city of Memphis by damming the Nile to reclaim land on which to build the royal stronghold. Memphis was to remain the administrative capital of Egypt for most of antiquity. While kings from time to time established residences elsewhere, it was at Memphis, conveniently situated at the natural division of Upper and Lower Egypt, that many of the offices of state resided.

A great cemetery was established adjacent to the new capital, the huge *mastaba* tombs of the nobility being erected on the edge of the escarpment, clearly visible from the town. Now known as Saqqara, the necropolis was to remain in use until the end of ancient Egyptian civilization, extending for many kilometres north and south of its First Dynasty core. The old view that these magnificent tombs were those of kings has now clearly been shown to be incorrect.

The kings, in fact, continued to be buried amongst their Predynastic ancestors at Abydos. The Horus Narmer and Horus Aha were interred directly south-west of cemetery U, as had been one or two of the kings who separated them from 'Scorpion'. That of Aha was a complex of three large, brick lined chambers (numbered B10/15/19), roofed over with wood, and possibly without any kind of superstructure. Some way to the east were a set of graves, whose young male occupants seem to have been sacrificed at the time of the king's interment. This barbarous practice of sending servants to join their master or mistress in the afterlife was to continue for only a few generations, and had died out by the end of the First Dynasty.

The monumental part of the tomb of the Horus Aha lay one and three quarter kilometres to the north-east, where a large rectangular enclosure of brick, with corner bastions and towers was erected, the earliest of a series of such monuments which complemented the burial chambers at Umm el-Qaab.

Horus Djer, Djet and Den

c. 2975-2875 BC

The Horus Aha's three successors' reigns saw the consolidation of the unified state. Under the Horus Djer, we have our first records of military expeditions outside the 'Two Lands'. In the east, forces were sent out into Sinai and perhaps beyond, one of the king's regnal years being named 'The Year of Smiting the land of the *Setjet*', a word later referring to Syria-Palestine.

There is also evidence for operations against the Libyans in the west; the Horus Djer's reign thus precurses the foreign concerns of his successors, over the next three millennia. Posterity regarded the king as something of a scholar, Manetho stating him to be the author of an anatomy text book, still extant in Greek times.

The king's wife seems to have been one Herneith, possibly buried at Saqqara in tomb 3507, alongside those of other senior figures of the period. The Horus Djer himself, however, was buried

Fig. 4. The Umm el-Qaab cemetery at Abydos, from the east. The mounds represent the debris from the work of various plunderers and excavators. The vast mass of potsherds left behind by these workers gives the site its Arabic name, 'Mother of Pots'.

at Umm el-Qaab, west of the tomb of the Horus Aha, in tomb O. Likewise a subterranean brick structure, containing a wooden inner chamber, it was much more elaborate than the sepulchres of his predecessors, with far more servant graves. Notably, the area between the chamber roof and the ground surface was occupied by a gravel tumulus, perhaps representing the primeval mound that played a large rôle in Egyptian creation myth. In Middle Kingdom times, the long-robbed tomb was identified as that of the god Osiris, and was equipped by a Thirteenth Dynasty king with a statue of the deity, lying on a bed. In the time of Amenophis III, and for many generations afterwards, it was a centre of pilgrimage. Through all this, a portion of the body of the king or his queen remained in the tomb, a part of an arm, hidden by a robber in a hole in the brick-work, near the entrance. It still bore four gold and turquoise bracelets, found in 1900 by Sir Flinders Petrie, and now

16

in Cairo; unhappily, the bones were discarded by an uncomprehending museum curator.

The second part of the Horus Djer's tomb lay near the Horus Aha's enclosure, a brick-walled monument, with the same panelled motif seen on the exteriors of the contemporary *mastabas* at Saqqara. It was surrounded by subsidiary graves, as was that of his successor, the Horus Djet, built directly west of it. These enclosures seem to have contained a complex of buildings in wood and other perishable materials.

The Horus Djet's body was also interred near his father(?)'s, in tomb Z at Umm el-Qaab, once again accompanied by his servants. The tomb was marked by a magnificent stela, bearing the king's name, and now in the Louvre. Of his reign, all that is known is that an expedition seems to have made its way to the Red Sea, perhaps to take ship for some more distant point.

It is possible that the Horus Djet may have died prematurely, since after him the rule of Egypt seems to have been exercised for some years by a woman named Meryetneith, possibly his widow. Her tomb at Umm el-Qaab (tomb Y) and enclosure to the northeast are indistinguishable from those of the kings, including the bodies of sacrificed retainers, and her sealings are found in a noble's tomb at Saqqara (3503). Most probably, she was acting as regent for a king too young to rule alone, probably the Horus Den, under whom she certainly died.

In keeping with his probable youth on accession, the Horus Den had a long reign, with many objects surviving from his time. His chancellor, Hemaka, is a well-known figure, and possessed an important tomb (3035) at Saqqara, whose contents provide us with our most comprehensive collection of First Dynasty funerary equipment. The king seems to have campaigned to the east, and celebrated a *Sed*-festival, or jubilee, an event that usually occurred after thirty years on the throne.

Like the Horus Djer, he left behind him an intellectual reputation, the discovery of spells in the later funerary manual, the *Book of the Dead*, being attributed to his time, as well as medical formulae preserved in New Kingdom papyri. More definitively attributable to the reign of the Horus Den is the earliest use of granite in a notable way, since the floor of his Abydene tomb (T) is paved with this material. This sepulchre is the most impressive of

17

Fig. 5. Two labels from the tomb of the Horus Den; the depictions upon them were intended to commemorate the key event of the year, as the earliest kings dated by named, not numbered, years. On the left is depicted the king's jubilee ceremonies. A key of this was his running around a marked-out course to prove his continuing energy, and this is shown in the top-right corner. He is also shown, wrapped in a cloack, in a shrine overlooking the course. The hieroglyphs to the left name the king, and his Chancellor, Hemaka; the latter's tomb is known at Saqqara. On the right is another label commemorating the 'smiting of the Easterners'. Both from Umm el-Qaab, tomb T.

its kind thus far, with a proper stairway, and a massive burial chamber, once roofed with wood. His funerary enclosure doubtless lay near those of his predecessors, but has not thus far been identified.

After the Horus Den's death, there is evidence for some trouble within the royal family, since the names of his successor, the Horus Adjib, together with those of Meryetneith, are erased on objects from the tomb of the next king, the Horus Semerkhet. Of the final king of the dynasty, the Horus Qaa, little is known, apart from the king's tomb at Abydos, and those of officials at Saqqara. The burning of some tombs of the First Dynasty has sometimes been attributed to troubles which followed the ending of this royal line.

Horus and Seth Khasekhemwy

c. 2690-2663 BC

The Second Dynasty is a period of extreme obscurity. The order of the first few kings is reasonably clear, but later in the dynasty things become much more uncertain, with definite signs of disorder, if not full-scale civil war. The first rulers had their tombs at Saqqara, but in the middle of the dynasty we find a king returning to Abydos for his burial place, building both a tomb and funerary enclosure. This monarch is also unusual in that, rather than employing a Horus name, he calls himself 'the Seth Peribsen', possibly having changed his epithet from the more conventional 'Horus Sekhemib'. Now, in later mythology, Seth is the enemy of Horus, and some have wondered whether this divine antipathy might have its origins in a conflict between this 'Seth-king' and the orthodox 'Horus-kings'.

That there may have been a period where the throne was disputed between two rival monarchs is suggested by the fact that a king named the Horus Khasekhem built at Hierakonpolis a funerary enclosure of the same kind as those at Abydos, suggesting an intention to be buried there. Hierakonpolis was perhaps the ancestral home of the Egyptian monarchy, and the building of the royal funerary monument there was presumably because of the non-availability of any more northerly necropolis. Warfare is also suggested by two statues of the king from the site, which show on their bases slaughtered bodies, labelled as representing 47,209 northern enemies. Other records indicate that fighting occurred in the territory of Hierakonpolis itself.

It is uncertain whether the Horus Khasekhem's enemy was the Seth Peribsen, or some other individual; in favour of the latter is the fact that the Seth Peribsen was considered a legitimate king by later generations. In any case, it was to the Horus Khasekhem that victory was granted, and it seems that magnanimity was felt to be the order of the day. This is intimated by the new form adopted for the king's *serekh*-name: rather than 'the Horus Khasekhem' ('Appearance of Power'), he is now 'the Horus and Seth Khasekhemwy' ('Appearance of Two Powers'), to which the further epithet *'Nebwy-hetep-im-ef'* ('the two lords are at peace in

19

him') is sometimes added. The king thus signalled that, whatever conflicts had been abroad, they were now over.

Having reunited the country, the Horus and Seth Khasekhemwy abandoned his Hierakonpolis funerary enclosure. However, rather than returning to the Saqqara burial place of the earliest kings of his line, he built his new tomb at Umm el-Qaab, together with a funerary enclosure alongside those of the First Dynasty kings – and the Seth-king, Peribsen.

Both monuments are the biggest of their respective types at the site. The underground tomb is no less than 68 metres long, by 12 broad, centring on a stone-built burial chamber, although these dimensions are insignificant when one compares them with those of the Saqqara tomb of the dynastic founder, the Horus Hetepsekhemwy, whose substructure occupies an area of 123 x 49 metres. Considerable quantities of material were recovered from the nearly sixty store-rooms, including a pair of servant-skeletons –

Fig. 6. The Shunet el-Zebib, *the funerary enclosure of the Horus and Seth Khasekhemwy at Abydos.*

20

the last known manifestation of the custom that had earlier surrounded the First Dynasty tombs with hundreds of such burials. The limestone walls of the burial chamber are the earliest of their kind known, with a number of substantial granite elements from other sites attesting to the building work carried out by the king.

The king's funerary enclosure, known today as the *Shunet el-Zebib* ('Storehouse of the Dates'), is by far the best preserved of its *genre* at Abydos, with its panelled walls still standing a number of metres above the desert surface. Recent excavations have told us rather more about the constructions that it held, most importantly, a mound of sand and rubble, covered with a skin of mud-brick, which could be the prototype for what was later to develop into the pyramid.

The Horus and Seth Khasekehmwy's wife seems to have been one Nimaethap; certainly, she was the mother of his immediate successors who were, however, later regarded as beginning a fresh dynasty. Accordingly, with Khasekhemwy we come to the end of the formative era of the Archaic Period, and move on into the first of the great periods of Egypt's history, the Old Kingdom.

IV The First Pyramid Builders

Djoser

c. 2663-2643 BC

Whatever the nature of the disturbances that seem to have beset the Second Dynasty, they had definitively ended before a new, Third, dynasty arose, in the person of the Horus Netjerykhet, better known by the name Djoser, perhaps his personal name, but only found on monuments dating from long after his death. The discovery of his sealings in the tomb of the Horus and Seth Khasekhemwy at Abydos has now proved that he did indeed found the dynasty, rather than being preceded by another king. That Djoser's reign was felt to be an important point in Egyptian history by New Kingdom scribes is indicated by the fact that his name is exceptionally inscribed in red ink in the Turin king list, a document written around the time of Ramesses II.

Djoser's parentage is uncertain, but it is likely that he was a son of Queen Nimaethap and the Horus and Seth Khasekhemwy. As with most of the early kings, very little is known of the events of his reign. He is depicted in the Sinai, while building work at Heliopolis is attested by some fragments of a shrine from there, which show the king, together with three of his women-folk – his mother(?) and two daughters, Hetephirnebty and Intkaes.

Of the activities of his reign, only an expedition to the mines of Sinai is properly attested by an inscription in the Wadi Maghara. The Sinai was later to be a source of copper ore, but in early times most of the work there seems to have been aimed at the acquisition of the greatly-prized semi-precious stone, turquoise. Djoser's inscription is the earliest monument to record such work, but those of subsequent reigns are plentiful, including depictions of his immediate successors, the Horus Sanakhte and Sekhemkhet.

Fig. 7. The limestone statue of King Djoser from the closed chamber (serdab) *of the mortuary temple of his pyramid at Saqqara.*

However, if a Ptolemaic stela at Sehel, near the First Cataract, could be believed, the reign will have seen a severe famine, ended by the ceding of land in the area to the cult of the god Khnum. Although a fiction, certainly composed for propagandistic purposes in the reign of Ptolemy V, two and a half millennia after the king's death, the text is interesting in that, in it, Djoser is made to consult one Imhotep.

23

This Imhotep was one of the few Egyptian commoners to attain divine status after his death, being renowned for his wisdom, and eventually, in Greek times, becoming a god of medicine and proclaimed a son of the Memphite god, Ptah. However, that his prominence extended back to the time of his royal master, Djoser, is indicated by the base of a statue of that king, where the name and titles of the Chancellor, &c, Imhotep, stand opposite those of Djoser in a manner that is quite exceptional for a commoner at any time. Of the myriad qualities that doubtless lay behind Imhotep's exalted place in the royal favour, only one can be verified today: that is his architectural genius, for to him may be attributed the construction of the world's first substantial stone building.

Stone had been used for various architectural elements during the Archaic Period, but the buildings themselves, no matter how huge, had been largely of mud brick. However, a few short years later there arose upon the desert plateau that rises above the site of the ancient capital of Memphis a structure over 62 metres high by 125 metres wide, surrounded by a huge enclosure with a bewildering complex of buildings – all built of hewn stone.

Fig. 8. The necropolis of Saqqara, with the Step Pyramid of King Djoser on the centre. The pyramids flanking it are the Fifth Dynasty monuments of Unas and Userkaf, respectively; together, they demonstrate the rise and decline of pyramid building, all within three centuries.

24

Fig. 9. Limestone statue-base of King Djoser, with the king's names and titles on the right, and those of his Chancellor and architect, Imhotep, on the left.

At first, all that was intended was an enlarged version of the Horus and Seth Khasekhemwy's *Shunet el-Zebib*, using limestone imitations of the bricks used there. The central massif, however, rather than being a simple brick-skinned mound, was made a more regular, square structure. This was gradually enlarged before the decision was taken to transform it into a stepped structure. At first given four tiers, the final edifice was formed of six deep steps, perhaps representing a stairway to heaven: thus came into existence the first pyramid, the ancestor of a series that would only come to an end nearly three millennia later.

The enclosure was equipped with all kinds of stone buildings, imitating the wooden structures that seem to have been contained by the Archaic Period funerary enclosures. These represented palaces and ritual edifices, intended for the use of the dead king, and included elements specific to the jubilee, which it was expected would still take place in the afterlife.

One way in which the enclosure differed from its Abydos prototypes was that, rather than being some kilometres away, the tomb chambers were actually under the central edifice, now known as the Step Pyramid. The burial chamber lay at the bottom of a shaft, and when investigated in the 1930s was found to contain the broken-up remains of Djoser's mummy; among the pieces recovered were the left foot, the upper right arm and shoulder, parts of the chest and elements of the spine. The corpse had been closely wrapped in fine linen, which had then been covered in plaster and moulded to the form of the underlying body. Since it has never proven possible to properly clear the chamber, it is probable that the rest of the king's body remains under the pyramid.

After Djoser, our knowledge of the royal succession becomes sketchy. He was probably succeeded by the Horus Sanakhte, formerly believed to be the dynastic founder and apparently the first monarch to use a cartouche for his personal name. Next seems to have come the Horus Sekhemkhet, who began a similar tomb-complex south-west of the Step Pyramid, apparently overseen by Imhotep himself, but the ordering of the next two or three kings is questionable, the ancient king lists indicating that there was a gap in the official records.

Seneferu

c. 2597-2547 BC

The last king of the Third Dynasty was Huni. His burial place is uncertain, but a strong the candidate is the Brick Pyramid at Abu Rowash, 25 kilometres north of Saqqara. He was succeeded by Seneferu, apparently the son of Meresankh I, presumably a wife of King Huni. Seneferu seems to have had a fairly large family, his eldest son, Nefermaet, becoming vizier, and probably only denied the succession by his premature death. He was possibly followed as vizier by another royal son, Kanefer, who was to serve on into the next reign. At least two daughters are known, besides other male offspring.

Events recorded from Seneferu's reign include expeditions against Libya and Nubia, 7,000 prisoners being claimed from the latter campaign. In addition, activity in the turquoise mines of the Sinai is indicated by a depiction from Wadi Maghara, showing the king smiting a local enemy. Another commodity-bearing activity was the import in a single year of forty ship-loads of cedar. These seem to have come from the port of Byblos in the Lebanon, which was for centuries Egypt's principal trading partner in that area.

One of the uses of the timber was in the construction of what was originally intended to be the king's burial place, the Bent Pyramid at Dahshur, a few kilometres south of the Step Pyramid. This was not, however, the only pyramid in whose construction Seneferu was involved, since he was certainly responsible for building three from scratch, and was party to building some, if not all, of a fourth. The latter monument was the pyramid at Meidum. This structure was begun as a step pyramid, but converted while still under construction into the first straight-edged, or 'true', pyramid, thus changing from a staircase to heaven into a representation of sun's rays. It is clear that a large proportion of the work at the site was carried out in the early years of Seneferu's reign, but it is uncertain whether it had been begun for him, or formed the tomb of his predecessor, Huni, which he piously undertook to complete.

No questions, however, surround his work at Dahshur. The Bent Pyramid had been intended from the outset to be a true pyramid, and had been half finished when a disaster seems to have occurred, the settling of the structure causing the opening of great cracks in the substructure and casing. A radical redesign added a strengthening layer to the outside of the pyramid, together with a new set of chambers; yet another alteration reduced its height by limiting the angle of the upper part – thus giving the monument its modern name.

None of these efforts, however, seem to have convinced the king that the building was a safe place to spend eternity, since the construction of a new pyramid was ordered, two kilometres further north. It was here, in the Red Pyramid, that the king was finally buried, parts of his mummy being found there in 1950. The body was that of a man past middle age, but not greatly so, suggesting that the king had come to the throne as a young man, since the

Fig. 10. Seneferu, on a limestone stela from the subsidiary pyramid of the Bent Pyramid at Dahshur.

evidence of graffiti on the pyramids suggests a reign approaching
half a century.

The final pyramid worked upon by Seneferu was a small one,
lacking a substructure. This was the step pyramid at Seila, ten
kilometres west of Meidum, finds from whose chapel included a
fragmentary statue and naos, a libation table, and two stelae, one
of which preserved Seneferu's names. The purpose of such miniature pyramids is unclear, although a number are extant, and all

seem to date to the very end of the Third Dynasty or beginning of the Fourth.

In view of the immense labour which must have accompanied Seneferu's pyramid-building activities (the two Dahshur monuments are the third and fourth biggest pyramids ever built), the king seems to have been remembered particularly fondly by posterity. In a number of literary works, he is depicted as a ruler who would address a commoner as 'my friend', 'my brother', or even 'comrade', and was not above doing his own note-taking; he is also referred to as 'The Beneficent King', an epithet used of no other monarch of old. Such sentiments are manifested in the popularity of his posthumous cult, surviving in some places for nearly three millennia, quite exceptionally for any king of his era.

Since the Archaic Period, there had been a steady development of the plastic arts, although in many cases only fragments have come to light. From Seneferu's reign, however, we have a number of fine pieces of sculpture in both two and three dimensions, amongst the latter being the portrait-statue of his son Rahotpe, a triumph of realism. We also have the set of furniture that accompanied the king's wife, Hetepheres I, to the grave. Almost entirely covered in gold leaf, it is of a superbly simple, yet effective design, alongside which many of the celebrated items of later times look tawdry.

Kheops

c. 2547-2524 BC

In contrast with the highly favourable reputation enjoyed by his father, Kheops, the son of Seneferu and Hetepheres, has suffered from a distinctly bad press at the hands of popular tradition. The view of him current in Late times was recorded by Herodotus:

> Kheops brought the country into all kinds of misery. He closed the temples, forbade his subjects to offer sacrifices, and compelled them without exception to labour upon his works.... The Egyptians can hardly bring themselves to mention ... Kheops ..., so great is their hatred ....

Fig. 11. The Great Pyramid at Giza; in the foreground are private tombs, and on the bottom left, the tomb of Queen Khentkaues I.

Stories written closer to his own time, while less extreme, also show the king's personality in a poor light, particularly when he appears in the same work as his father.

It is impossible to know how far this view corresponds to reality. It has been suggested that the episode of closing temples is taken from the later iconoclastic actions of the heretic king Akhenaten (see p.104, below), referred by folk-memory into the distant past, but one has little difficulty in identifying the root-cause of the view of Kheops as a megalomaniac tyrant – his tomb.

This monument, the Great Pyramid at Giza, was for countless years the largest building in the world, and still one of the most stupendous works of mankind, 230 metres square and 147 metres high. It was doubtless such statistics that influenced the popular view of the builder – ignoring the fact that the aggregate labour carried out for Seneferu at Dahshur, Meidum and Seila far exceeded that of Kheops at Giza.

The pyramid and its adjoining buildings followed a basic layout established by the monuments of Seneferu. The great encl-

30

Fig. 12. The Sinai quarrying inscription of Kheops.

osure and contained buildings that Djoser and his immediate
successors had taken over from the Abydene structures of the
Archaic Period were replaced by a simpler scheme: against the
eastern face of the pyramid stood the mortuary temple; from this,
a causeway led east to a 'valley building' on the edge of the desert
plateau, connected to the Nile by a canal. Besides these elements
there was a small subsidiary pyramid (in Kheops' case only
recently located), of uncertain ritual import, and a series of pits
intended for the boats employed in the funeral ceremonies.

The Great Pyramid itself underwent a number of constructional phases, apparently resulting from a late decision to employ a
stone sarcophagus. This meant that a chamber deep underground,
approached by a long corridor, only a metre square, was
abandoned in favour of burial apartments high up in the body of

the pyramid itself. There, the sarcophagus could be put in place and the sepulchral room built round it. Later pyramids had much shallower substructures, with their main chambers left open to the sky until the lower courses of the pyramid were built over them.

Concerning the 'real' Kheops, little evidence survives; he is attested in the Sinai, and worked the diorite quarries that lie deep in the Nubian desert, north-west of Abu Simbel. For much of his reign the vizierate was in the hands of his kinsman, Hemiun, son of Nefermaet. Many members of the royal family are known from the huge cemetery of mastabas that was laid out around the royal pyramid, the heir being apparently Kawab, son of the senior wife, Merityotes. This lady was presumably buried in one of the three small pyramids built for the king's mother and wives just south of the mortuary temple of the main pyramid, and west of the recently-uncovered subsidiary pyramid. Other sons included Khufukhaf, Minkhaf and Djedefhor, besides the later kings, Djedefre and Khephren. Djedefhor was later highly regarded as a wise man, and a fragment of one of his writings still survives. A number of these sons feature as story tellers in a cycle of tales set at the court of Kheops, known today from Papyrus Westcar.

Kheops was succeeded by Djedefre, whom some have claimed to be a usurper, but with little certainty. He carried out the funeral ceremonies of his father, his name appearing on the covering blocks of one of the aforementioned funerary boat-pits. After a fairly short reign, during which he built a pyramid at Abu Rowash, he was apparently succeeded by his brother Khephren, although it has been suggested that a further ruler was interposed between them. He may have been the son whom Djedefre is known to have possessed, but the evidence remains equivocal.

Mykerinos

c. 2493-2475 BC

Khephren suffers from a similar reputation to Kheops, as one who closed the temples to provide labourers for his Second Pyramid at

Giza, which approaches that of his father's in size. In contrast, his son, Mykerinos is reported by Herodotus as having

> of all the kings who ruled Egypt, ... the greatest reputation for justice ... and for this the Egyptians give him higher praise than any other monarch.

One cannot help but speculate that this reputation flowed from the smaller size of Mykerinos' Third Pyramid as compared to those of Kheops and Khephren, which tower above it on the Giza plateau.

There is some later evidence for one or two kings interposing themselves between Khephren and his son, presumably as a continuation of the putative power-struggle that had followed the death of Kheops three decades earlier. However, the contemporary material does not provide secure corroboration for such an occurrence, and it remains quite possible that Mykerinos succeeded Khephren directly.

The events of the reign of Mykerinos are little-known. A number of members of the court have been identified, including the viziers, Iunmin and Nebemakhet, who were the king's brothers, along with other siblings, one of whom, Sekhemkare, was to live to serve no fewer than five pharaohs.

Mykerinos was married to his sister, Khamerernebty II, the couple having at least two children, Princes Khuenre and, presumably, Shepseskaf, Mykerinos' eventual successor. Khuenre, the original heir to the throne, died before his father, and was buried in a rock-tomb (MQ 1), south-east of his father's pyramid. Interestingly enough, the queen was not buried near her husband, but instead close to the valley building of the funerary complex of her father, Khephren. Mykerinos would seem to have had at least two other wives, given the presence of a pair of small pyramids alongside his complex's subsidiary example; one of them contained the skeleton of a young woman.

The king's funerary complex was still under construction at the time of his death. Much of the granite which he had uniquely used to cover the lower quarter of the pyramid still awaited dressing, while the temples were still far from complete, to be hurriedly finished off in brick by the new king, Shepseskaf. The pyramid chambers had, like those of the Great Pyramid, undergone considerable modification before Mykerinos was interred within, in a wonderful basalt sarcophagus, decorated with the elaborate panelled motif that had first appeared on the First Dynasty *mastabas* at Saqqara.

How long he lay there undisturbed is unknown; two millennia after Mykerinos' funeral, however, Twenty-sixth Dynasty priests entered the pyramid and placed what remained of his mummy in a new wooden coffin. This coffin was found again in AD 1837, smashed and buried under the metre of debris that had accumulated in the pyramid antechamber. Next to it were the legs and lower torso of a human body, together with a foot and some ribs and vertebrae, all enclosed in a layer of dried skin, and a few scraps of cloth.

Although the archaeological evidence would seem to point to these being the last sorry remnants of Mykerinos, radiocarbon tests appear to indicate that they are at most only 1,650 years old. There is, however, a possibility of contamination at the time of the pyramid's final robbery, or since discovery, leaving the question still open. The remains now repose in the British Museum, along with the Saite coffin; however, the sarcophagus now lies on the bed of the sea, off the Spanish coast, where sank the ship in which it was being carried to England.

V The Openers of the Ways

Sahure

c. 2464-2452 BC

Shepseskaf was the last king of the Fourth Dynasty, reigning for
only four years and forsaking a pyramid for a low, rectangular
monument at South Saqqara, known as the *Mastabat Faraoun*.
His immediate successor seems to have been Userkaf, regarded as
the founder of the Fifth Dynasty, and a grandson of King Djedefre
by his daughter, Neferhetepes.

He was followed by Sahure, the first of two sons of Queen
Khentkaues I to hold the throne. It is generally assumed that this
lady was married to Userkaf, but he is nowhere mentioned in the
oddly-shaped tomb she built at Giza – twenty kilometres away
from Userkaf's pyramid at Saqqara. In at least one relief she
seems to wear the royal uraeus and beard, perhaps indicating a
period during which she was regent of the kingdom. From this
circumstance, one can probably infer that Khentkaues was a scion
of the branch of the Fourth Dynasty represented by the Giza-
pyramid builders, Khephren and Mykerinos. Perhaps her union
with Djedefre's grandson brought to an end the dynastic frictions
that seem to have beset the heirs of Kheops.

In this connection, it is interesting to note that a Middle
Kingdom folk-tale makes the first three kings of the Fifth Dynasty
the children of the son god, Re, born of Reddjedet, wife of Reuser, a
priest of Re. While this cannot be squared with the contemporary
evidence, the motif of the physical siring of the future king by the
paramount god is one which we will meet again in the New
Kingdom.

The Fifth and Sixth Dynasties seem to have been periods of
fairly extensive state-sponsored foreign enterprises, both peaceful
and otherwise. Under Sahure, we have depictions of the return of

Fig. 13. *King Sahure smites his foes: rock inscription from the Wadi Maghara, Sinai.*

ships from a voyage to the Lebanese port of Byblos, from which source probably derive the bears shown in another relief. We also have the first recorded expedition to the territory of Punt, in the penultimate year of the king's reign, which yielded considerable quantities of myrrh.

Punt lay on the coast of the Red Sea, covering parts of the modern Sudan, Eritrea and Ethiopia. Access to it involved the building of ships on Egypt's Red Sea coast, and then sailing around a thousand kilometres southwards. On the return journey, once Egyptian waters had been reached, goods had to be unloaded and carried along the Eastern Desert roads until the Nile was regained. In New Kingdom times, this transshipment occurred through the Wadi Hammamat, but it has been suggested that in the Old Kingdom it may have taken place far further north, perhaps from the area of Suez.

Like many of his predecessors, Sahure left a relief at the Sinai turquoise quarries, and also worked the Nubian diorite quarries, following the example of kings back to at least Kheops. A temple-scene commemorates a raid into Libya which yielded various livestock and showed the king smiting the local chieftain who had stood in his way. Curiously, the scene was used in the mortuary temple of Pepy II *and* in a Kawa temple of Taharqa, nearly two thousand years later, with the same names quoted for the chief and his family, making one suspicious as to whether the Sahure depiction is wholly accurate, or itself a copy of an even earlier representation!

During the Fourth Dynasty, the vizierate was largely in the hands of the royal princes; under the Fifth, this was no longer the case, since Sekhemkare, Khephren's son and office-holder at the beginning of Sahure's reign, was followed by a series of commoners. Officials maintained royal links, the High Priest of Ptah, Ptah-shepses, marrying a daughter of Shepseskaf, but no longer did kings' sons aspire to major posts in the administration, a situation that was to last until well into the New Kingdom.

A feature of the Fifth Dynasty kings is their building of a sun temple, as well as a pyramid; the former comprised a bulky obelisk, a chapel, and a causeway. The first example, that of Userkaf, was erected at Abusir, about four kilometres north of the Step Pyramid. That of Sahure was named *Sekhet-Re*, 'the Field of Re', but its location has yet to be established for certain. It probably lay a little north of Userkaf's, given that the temple of Sahure's second successor lay about a kilometre further north, at Abu Ghurob.

Fig. 14. The pyramid of King Sahure at Abusir: view up the causeway to the entrance of the mortuary temple.

37

The area of Abusir was also chosen by Sahure for his pyramid. His monument marks the beginning of the real decline in pyramid building, both from the point of view of size and quality: he attempted to make up for this in the increased size and adornment of the adjoining mortuary temples. The Great Pyramid of Kheops had been 230 metres square, and built of massive stone blocks; Mykerinos' tomb had been built likewise, on a 108 metre base; Sahure's, on the other hand, was of small, badly formed stones, and only 78 metres square. Today, it bears only a passing resemblance to the pyramid form, the fine limestone casing having long been removed for reuse; the interior was also devastated by stone robbers, so that today one crawls with some difficulty into a cavity that once formed part of the burial chamber.

Sahure was succeeded by his brother Kakai (Neferirkare), the first king known to have employed a separate prenomen and nomen. He was buried at Abusir, as were his immediate successors, his son, Neferefre, and the rather better-attested Niuserre. Of uncertain antecedents was Shepseskare, perhaps Neferefre's successor, who probably began a pyramid at Abusir which was barely begun. Their successors, Menkauhor, Isesi and Unas, however, moved back to Saqqara, the last of them introducing religious texts to the walls of the royal burial chamber.

Exploitation of the minerals of the Sinai continued, as did other royal activities, but subtle changes are to be seen from the reign of Isesi onwards. Most obvious is the end to sun-temple building, but there were also alterations in the system of ranking titles bestowed upon the nobility; additionally, the banishment of royal sons from the senior administration was temporarily ended. Perhaps most significant was the recognition of the status of the provinces by the appointment of more than one vizier, one of whom was based in the southern part of the country.

The latter part of the Old Kingdom is characterised by the increase in the number and quality of the tombs built at provincial centres by local dignitaries, in particular by the nome-governors, or nomarchs. This factor becomes most noticeable in the Sixth Dynasty, which was traditionally regarded as having begun at the death of Unas, although there is no real evidence for a break in the royal line at this point. A possible point of significance, however, is a depiction within the royal funerary complex of Unas of persons affected by famine. If Egyptians, their state might indicate the effect of the troubles within the country that could have influenced a change in dynasty. On the other hand, the relief – found out of any obvious context – may depict foreigners, to whom pharaoh's generosity is bringing succour: as with so many pieces of evidence for Egyptian history, we just do not know.

Pepy I

c. 2343-2297 BC

The first king of the new, Sixth, dynasty was Teti, who was ultimately followed on the throne by his son by Queen Iput I, Pepy I. It is possible that a King Userkare reigned briefly between the two, but there is little evidence outside later King Lists.

During the first half of his reign, Pepy I used the prenomen Nefersahor, but changed it later to Meryre; such changes are known at other points in Egyptian history (e.g. Montjuhotpe II, Siptah, Ramesses IV), but are of uncertain significance. His long tenure of the throne saw expeditions sent south and east, the latter both to the mines of Sinai and further afield, into southern Palestine. These operations were led by Uni, a native of the area of El-Kab, and are the earliest certain records of penetration into that area. They involved the landing of troops from the sea before proceeding into the highlands where the people who were the object of this apparently-punitive campaign were to be found.

Uni also records in his autobiography, from Abydos, that he was responsible for the prosecution of an unnamed wife of the king; nothing more is known about the affair, but it is instructive to note that both of the sons who followed Pepy I on the throne were born of ladies married to the king two decades into his reign. One can only assume some form of harim-intrigue in the fall-out from which the offspring of the prosecuted elder wife were disinherited or worse. Another victim seems to have been the vizier, Rewer, whose names have been erased from his tomb, and from at least one royal inscription.

The first 'new' wife taken by the king was Ankhnesmeryre I,

by her name either born during her husband's reign, or re-named in his honour. She was the sister of Djau, an offspring of provincial nobility from the area of Abydos, who was later to be appointed a southern vizier. The queen was to become the mother of the Crown Prince, Nemtyemsaf, but it appears that she died some years before the king, being replaced by her sister, Ankhnesmeryre II. This lady was to bear the king his younger son, Pepy, a short time before, or even after, Pepy I's death. A further series of wives were revealed by the discovery in the early 1990s of a number of small pyramids adjacent to that of the king himself.

Evidence of the king's building activities comes from a number of sites: the remains of a chapel survive at Bubastis, with other elements coming from Aswan (Elephantine) and Abydos. A text in a crypt in the Ptolemaic temple at Dendara suggests that he also carried out work there. A once-fine copper statue of Pepy I was recovered at Hierakonpolis, attesting to his involvement there as well: a superb gold falcon's head from the same place, part of the cult-image of the god Horus, may also date to his reign.

Pepy I built his pyramid at South Saqqara. Like those of Unas and Teti, it was decorated with the magical Pyramid Texts, intended to smooth the dead king's way to eternity. Some mutilations of his name suggest some kind of posthumous antipathy against him, but the worst damage to the tomb was carried out by stone-robbers of the Middle Ages. When entered by Flinders Petrie in 1880, all that seems to have survived of the king's mummy were a few bandages – and a single hand.

Pepy II

c. 2290-2196 BC

Pepy I was succeeded by his elder son, Nemtyemsaf I, who may have previously served as his father's coregent for a period of years. His relatively short reign saw further activities by his father's old retainer, Uni, and the first of a number of African expeditions by Harkhuf, the governor of Aswan. The interest now being shown by the pharaohs is illustrated by Nemtyemsaf's visit to Aswan in his ninth regnal year to receive a group of southern chieftains.

Fig. 15. Harkhuf and his son; on one African expedition, he obtained a dancing deneg *that delighted his child-king, Pepy II; tomb A.8 at Aswan (Qubbet el-Hawa).*

Nemtyemsaf's sudden death, when still a young man, brought his brother Pepy II to the throne while yet a child. Power lay in the hands of his mother, Ankhnesmeryre II, and his uncle Djau, now southern vizier. Under their charge, the extensive foreign ventures of Harkhuf and other Aswan dignitaries continued apace, extending far into the African continent in search of trade items.

On three previous occasions, Harkhuf had visited the land of Yam, probably lying in the area to the south of modern Khartoum. His fourth journey took place not long after Pepy II's accession, and during it he acquired a dancing *deneg* – either a pygmy or a dwarf. This fact was included in a report sent ahead to Egypt while he undertook the northward journey back to Egypt. The idea of the *deneg* clearly delighted the boy-king, who commanded Harkhuf to:

41

Come northwards to the residence immediately; you should bring this *deneg* with you, which you have brought living, prosperous and healthy from the land of the horizon-dwellers, for the dances of the god, to gladden the heart of the Dual King Neferkare (Pepy II) .... When he goes down with you into the ship, appoint worthy people to be around him on deck: take care lest he fall in the water! When he lies down at night, appoint worthy people to lie around him in his tent: inspect ten times a night! My person desires to see this *deneg* more than all the products of the Sinai and Punt!

Harkhuf clearly completed his commission, being so pleased with his king's letter that he included it in the autobiographical text that adorns the façade of his tomb at Qubbet el-Hawa, Aswan.

Other Aswan-based desert travellers included Sabni, who journeyed into Nubia to recover the body of his father, Mekhu, one of many who had found death while seeking the exotic products of the south. Pepynakhte, also called Heqaib, made two military expeditions into Nubia, before being sent into the eastern desert to recover the body of a colleague who had been murdered by local tribesmen while building a boat on the Red Sea coast in preparation for a trip to Punt. He succeeded in this task, as well as punishing those responsible for the killing. Of particular interest is the fact that in the years after his death, Heqaib became a god, worshipped in a chapel on the island of Elephantine which drew royal patronage for many generations.

Having come to the throne young, Pepy II lived on – and on! It is generally accepted that he reigned for no fewer than ninety-four years, although it has been suggested that this should be reduced to sixty-four. During that period he was served by some ten viziers, and married at least four wives, Neith, Iput II, Udjebten and Ankhnespepy. All of the latter were buried around the king's pyramid at South Saqqara, the last of the large royal tombs of the Old Kingdom. The king was succeeded by his son, Nemtyemsaf II, mentioned as Crown Prince on a stela from Queen Neith's pyramid-complex. The new pharaoh's reign was, however, short, and before long, Egypt was sliding towards disunion and, ultimately, civil war.

VI   Collapse and Recovery

'Nitokris'

c. 2190 BC

The years following the death of Pepy II are amongst the most obscure in Egyptian history, since Nemtyemsaf II's short reign was followed by a series of rulers whose number and order are distinctly unclear. Pepy II's widow, Ankhnespepy, is known to have been the mother of a king Neferkare, and was buried either by him or another in one of the store-rooms of Queen Iput II's mortuary chapel. That such a burial-place was not unusual at this time is shown by the mummy of Prince Ptahshepses, interred in a second-hand sarcophagus in the valley temple of Unas.

Amongst these obscure monarchs is the legendary Nitokris, allegedly the second woman (after Meryetneith) to act as King of Egypt. Herodotus tells us that:

> She killed hundreds of Egyptians to avenge the king, her brother, whom his subjects had killed, and had forced her to succeed. This she did by constructing a huge underground chamber, in which ... she invited to a banquet all those she knew to be chiefly responsible for her brother's death. Then, when the banquet was underway, she let the river in on them, through a concealed pipe .... After this fearful revenge, she flung herself into a room full of embers, to escape her punishment.

Unfortunately, there is no real evidence for such a lady ever having existed outside such folk-tales. However, while no doubt a fable, the skulduggery recounted may well reflect what lay behind the rapid changes of monarch that characterizes this, and other similar periods of history. A text composed somewhat closer to the apparent date of the events it purports to report (*The Admonitions of Ipuwer*, dating to the Middle Kingdom) suggests that not only was assassination abroad, but more far-reaching disorder:

> Lo, the face is pale, the bowmen ready,
> Crime is everywhere, there is no man of yesterday ...
> Lo, Hapy inundates and none plough for him,
> All say, "We know not what has happened to the land" ...
> Lo, poor men have become men of wealth,
> He who could not buy sandals now owns riches ...
> Lo, hearts are violent, a storm sweeps the land,
> Blood is everywhere, there is no shortage of dead ...
> Lo, many dead are buried in the river,
> The stream is the grave, the grave is the stream,
> Lo, nobles lament, the poor rejoice,
> Every town says, "Let us expel our rulers"...
> See now, men rebel against the Serpent,
> Stolen is the crown of Re, who pacifies the Two Lands ...
> See the royal residence is fearful from want ...
> The troops we raised for ourselves have become Bowmen, bent on destroying!

Another text (*The Prophesy of Neferti*, from the reign of Ammenemes I) paints a similar picture of the century or two following the fall of the Sixth Dynasty:

> I show you a land topsy-turvy!
> The weakly-armed is the strongly-armed,
> One salutes him who saluted ...
> The beggar will gain riches ...
> The slaves will be exalted.

Nitokris is usually regarded either as the last ruler of the Sixth Dynasty, or an early one of the Seventh/Eighth – best regarded as a single entity. Many of the kings of this dynasty are only known from the King List in the temple of Sethos I at Abydos. Of those who have some form of independent attestation, Ibi had a pyramid at Saqqara. Although decorated with Pyramid Texts, it is but a pale shadow of the great pyramids of the Old Kingdom: only 31 metres square, its pitiful remains crouch in the desert, half way down the causeway of the pyramid-complex of Pepy II.

The last three kings of the dynasty are known from decrees they issued in favour of Shemay and his son, Idy, at Koptos. The terms of these documents reflect the power of the local magnates, which had been increasing since Fifth Dynasty times: they successively obtained the dignities of Nomarch, Governor of Upper Egypt, and Vizier. By his marriage to the daughter of King Nefer-kahor, Shemay cemented his position in the state.

That state, however, was tottering on the edge of the abyss. It is by no means certain what lay at the heart of the malaise; a possibility is that a series of inadequate inundations had under-mined the national economy. Whatever the root cause, however, within a few years of the fall of the Sixth Dynasty, the authority of the Memphite pharaoh had become little more than nominal in many parts of the country, the power in at least the southern part of Egypt devolving to provincial – nome – level. It was only a matter of time before one of the nome-chieftains (nomarchs) felt himself able to challenge Memphis for the throne itself.

Akhtoy I-V

c. 2160-2040 BC

The challenge – by all indications a successful one – came from Akhtoy, the ruler of Herakleopolis, just south of the fertile Fayoum basin, and 90 kilometres from Memphis. The violence that surrounded his seizure of authority is reflected in Manetho's description of him as 'more terrible than his predecessors', who 'wrought evil things for those in all Egypt'.

Akhtoy may have initially gained power as far as Aswan in the south, but the Herakleopolitans' rule seems after a while to have become restricted to the territory north of the area of Abydos, the southern nomes banding together under the leadership of the hitherto-minor city of Thebes.

Although the Ninth/Tenth Dynasty of Akhtoy I and his successors acted as nominal overlords, the actual governance of the Nile valley was essentially feudal, with the local magnates regularly jockeying for position. Some formally acknowledged their loyalty to the royal house, but some nomarchs went as far as to date events by their own years of office, rather than by their king's regnal years.

Under Akhtoy's second successor, Neferkare, Ankhtify, the nomarch of Hierakonpolis, based at Mo'alla, less than 30 kilometres south of Thebes, led a coalition of his own and the Edfu nomes against the Thebans. This presumably constituted a pre-emptive strike against a polity that was already showing signs of challenging Ankhtify's Herakleopolitan overlords for dominance.

This was but the first episode of a conflict that was to last as long as the House of Akhtoy. Some decades later, the nomarch Tefibi of Asyut tells of how he fought against the Thebans and their allies, presumably the same campaign which is referred to by his king, Akhtoy V, in an instruction addressed to his heir. In it he regrets that his troops, having regained the Abydene area from the Thebans, set about plundering the ancient cemetery.

The Herakleopolitan success was apparently short-lived, the Thebans regaining the territory and agreeing some kind of truce by the time the throne had passed to Akhtoy V's son, Merykare. The alliance with Asyut remained strong, the king attending the installation of Tefibi's son, Akhtoy, in person. Nevertheless, fighting once again broke out around Abydos, with the fall of the Herakleopolitan kingdom occurring not long after the death of Merykare, and his burial in an as-yet unidentified pyramid at Saqqara, known only from textual references.

Inyotef II

c. 2123-2074 BC

The Theban regime that opposed the kings of the Ninth/Tenth Dynasty seems to trace its origins back to the local governors of the Upper Egyptian town in the Sixth Dynasty, or even the earlier dignitaries of the Fourth Dynasty who were responsible for a pair of large brick *mastabas* there. However, the real rise of the city seems to stem from the accession of one Inyotef, son of Ikui, to the nomarchy in the earlier years of the Ninth/Tenth Dynasty.

*Fig. 16. Kings Inyotef I, II & III, from a memorial
erected by Montjuhotpe II in the temple at Tod.*

He, or his immediate predecessor, had at an early stage made
common cause with Koptos which, as the ally of the now-exting-
uished Eighth Dynasty, could not have been overly friendly
towards the new Herakleopolitan kingdom. As we have seen, the
alliance rapidly came to blows with its southern neighbour, Ankhtify. A Theban settlement was destroyed in this fighting, but
within a few years the whole of southern Egypt was under the
control of the nomarch of Thebes, Inyotef now calling himself Great
Chief of Upper Egypt.

47

The following decades seem to have seen endemic fighting, combining with famine to produce miserable conditions throughout the country. At first, the Theban rulers were content with the status of particularly exalted nomarchs, but either during the tenure of Montjuhotpe I, or his successor, Inyotef I, they became kings, with Horus-names and single cartouches, although as yet no prenomina.

Inyotef II would appear to have been a brother of Inyotef I, and was responsible for the addition of the Thinite (Abydene) nome to his patrimony:

> [I made] its northern boundary as far as the Aphroditopolitan nome. I landed in the sacred valley (= Abydos), I captured the entire Thinite nome, I opened all its fortresses, I made it the gateway to the north.

The campaigns that brought about this result are mentioned in the autobiographies of a number of Inyotef II's henchmen. One, Djari, recounts how he 'fought with the House of Akhtoy on the west of Thinis'.

The latter years of Inyotef II's reign seem to have been those of truce with the Herakleopolitans, allowing the king to undertake building work and trade with both north and south. Part of his autobiography survives on the lower part of a great stela which was placed in his tomb. This was built on the West Theban plain at a place now known as El-Tarif, opposite the spot where lay the embryonic temple of the local god, Amun. This shrine, at Karnak, would one day become the largest religious structure in the world.

The king's tomb was a great courtyard, around 300 x 74 metres, surrounded by doorways that gave access to the tomb-chapels of favoured members of his entourage. At the back, a colonnade gave access to Inyotef II's own decorated offering-place and tomb-shaft, the whole structure being modelled on that of his predecessor, that lay a little way to the south. The stela lay in a structure at the front of the courtyard, perhaps a kind of valley building. Besides the autobiographical text, it bears a large standing figure of the king, together with images of five of his dogs, each of which is named. The Egyptians are well-known for their affection for animals, but it is most unusual to find a king placing his favourite pets on his funerary stela. It was accordingly a very real dog-lover who 'journeyed to the horizon' after fifty years in which he had set Thebes well on the way to the leadership of the country, a leadership she was to maintain for many of the remaining seventeen centuries of ancient Egyptian civilization.

Montjuhotpe II

c. 2066-2014 BC

Inyotef II's successor, Inyotef III, had a fairly short reign, during which the truce with Herakleopolis was maintained, and support provided during some kind of problem, perhaps a famine, that occurred in the Abydene region. He was followed on the Theban throne by his son, Montjuhotpe II, under whom peace was initially maintained. In his fourteenth regnal year, however, the Herakleopolitans, or their allies, attempted to re-take the Thinite nome, which had by now been a Theban possession for some decades.

This was a major mistake on the part of the 'House of Akhtoy', for its effect was to spell the end of the Ninth/Tenth Dynasty regime. During the years of fighting that ensued, Montjuhotpe II's forces drove steadily northwards, the Herakleopolitan armies apparently looting formerly friendly cities as they retreated. Asyut was taken and then Herakleopolis itself, leaving the absorbtion of the far north into the Theban kingdom simply a matter of time.

The bodies of some sixty soldiers found buried in Deir el-Bahari tomb MMA 507 have generally been regarded as being troops of Montjuhotpe killed in battle with the Herakleopolitans. They had all died in battle – killed outright by arrows, or given the *coup de grâce* while lying disabled on the ground. This dating has now been questioned, with the possibility that they may date to the early Twelfth Dynasty. Nevertheless, their interment in a tomb that lay alongside the sepulchres of such dignitaries as the Great Steward Henenu, the Vizier, Ipi, and a royal chancellor, indicates their importance and that of the nameless battle in which they fell — whether against the Herakleopolitans or some other foe of Pharaoh.

Fig. 17. The painted sandstone statue of King Montjuhotpe II, from his jubilee cenotaph at Deir el-Bahari. The dummy tomb is known as the Bab el-Hosan ('Gate of the Horse'), after its discovery, when the mount of the archaeologist Howard Carter stumbled above its entrance.

50

To mark his victory, Montjuhotpe adopted a prenomen and new Horus-name: up until then, the Theban rulers had contented themselves with but one cartouche-name. His titulary was once more revised some years later, the Horus-name becoming *Sematawy*, 'Uniter of the Two Lands'. The occasion of this change may have been the final recognition of the king as the undisputed ruler of the whole of Egypt, which would thus have been complete by the thirties' of the reign. This achievement was well remembered by posterity: in later inscriptions, Montjuhotpe II was set alongside Menes as being the second founder of the Egyptian state.

Having secured the country internally, the king soon began to extend his influence beyond its borders, undertaking police actions in the surrounding deserts and penetrating southwards into Nubia. Some kind of expedition into the southlands is apparently commemorated by an impressive series of reliefs at Shatt er-Rigal, near Gebel Silsila, while a number of texts record the military operations that aimed at restoring Egyptian control over the area upstream of Aswan.

It seems that the preceding period had seen the appearance of a quasi-Egyptian polity centred around the area of Abu Simbel, the names of a number of kings being found in this area, together with those of their followers, who appear to be of Egyptian origin. Montjuhotpe's forces moved against this southern state, and by regaining control over the area below the Second Cataract laid the foundations for the campaigns of the kings of the next, Twelfth, Dynasty. Year 41 saw the arrival at Aswan of a large fleet from Lower Nubia, led by none other than the Chancellor, Khety, illustrating the interest shown in re-opening Egypt's access to Nubia and beyond.

By now, the king had celebrated his jubilee, presumably on the thirtieth anniversary of his accession, which was the usual, but not invariable, occasion for such a festival. As part of the ceremonies, a dummy burial was made near the king's intended tomb: a painted statue of Montjuhotpe II, wearing Jubilee robes, was wrapped in linen and placed alongside an empty coffin at the end of a passage-way, 150 metres long and descending steeply into the bed-rock, now known as the Bab el-Hosan. Below that room, a shaft 30 metres deep gave access to another cavity, containing models of boats.

Fig. 18. King Montjuhotpe II, embraced by Re; from the rear part of his temple at Deir el-Bahari.

52

Montjuhotpe II built extensively, in particular in the area occupied by the original Theban kingdom. Fragments of his works survive at a number of sites, but his most impressive monument is the mortuary temple he erected at Deir el-Bahari at Western Thebes. The complex began with a long causeway up from the edge of the desert, flanked at its upper end by trees and statues of the king. At its end lay a terraced building, generally agreed now to have been surmounted by a replica of the 'primeval mound' from which all creation stemmed. Furnished with colonnades and pillared halls, it was extensively decorated with scenes of religion and warfare. From it derives much of our knowledge of the king's family.

The king's principal wife was named Tem, buried close alongside her husband, but he had a number of lesser consorts. A number of them died young in the first half of the reign: at least one, Henhenet, perished in childbirth. They were buried below dainty shrines behind the king's temple's central mound, only fragments of which now survive A second major wife was Neferu, the mother of the heir to the throne. She received a superbly decorated sepulchre just outside the temple, which remained a tourist-attraction into the New Kingdom, a special visitors' entrance being built when the original doorway was blocked by new constructional work under Hatshepsut.

The tombs of the nobles of the reigns of the Inyotefs had lined the long sides of the courtyard (*saff*) tombs in which the kings had been buried. Montjuhotpe's lined the sides of the great rock-bay that contained the royal mortuary temple. The king himself was interred at the end of another 150-metre passage, this time lying in the courtyard at the back of his temple. The sepulchral chamber, dominated by a huge alabaster shrine, was robbed in antiquity. Apart from fragments of coffin, canopics and wooden models, it revealed some pieces of the skull and half the lower jaw of the ruler, which were presented by the excavators to the British Museum.

After a reign of over half a century, the king was succeeded by his son and namesake, Montjuhotpe III. He continued the work of his father, before being in turn followed by a fourth King Montjuhotpe, with whom the Eleventh Dynasty was to come to an end. Apart from the reunification of the country, the period is important for raising the town of Thebes from a minor provincial centre to the status of royal residence. It also marked the beginning of the ascent of the god Amun from local deity to all-powerful King of the Gods, a process which, however, was not to become complete for another four centuries.

VII   The Seizers of the Two Lands

Ammenemes I

c. 1994-1964 BC

The Vizier and Governor of Upper Egypt under Montjuhotpe IV was named Amenemhat – 'Amun-is-foremost'. In the second year of the king's reign, he led a large expedition to the Wadi Hammamat, lying between Koptos and the Red Sea, to obtain stone for the king's sarcophagus. Inscriptions in the wadi record some of the remarkable events that occurred during this operation:

> There came a gazelle great with young, going with her face before her, while her eyes looked backwards. She did not turn back, and arrived at this august moment, at this block, still in its place, that was intended to be the lid of the sarcophagus. She dropped her young upon it while the army of the king looked on. They sacrificed her upon the block, and made a fire.

With the encouragement of this omen, the block was safely quarried for its journey to Thebes. Now, the Eastern Desert is a fairly arid place, with water only to be found at certain long-used wells; accordingly, another apparently miraculous event was judged worthy of commemoration:

> While working on the sarcophagus-block, the wonder was repeated. Rain was made, and the form of this god appeared, his fame was shown to the men, the highland being made into a lake .... A well was found in the midst of the valley, 10 cubits [5.2 metres] by 10 cubits on each side, filled with fresh water to its edge, undefiled, kept pure and cleansed from gazelles, concealed from barbarians. Soldiers of old and kings who had lived in the past had gone out and returned past it, but no eye had seen it, but ... (now) it was revealed.

The vizierate was the highest office to which a non-royal Egyptian could normally aspire. However, five years after his expedition to Hammamat, Amenemhat had achieved more: as Ammenemes I, he was now pharaoh.

Nothing is known of the means by which Ammenemes acquired the throne from Montjuhotpe IV. He may have staged a *coup d'etat* or, like certain other figures in Egyptian history, been nominated to succeed a childless monarch. The former option might be favoured if a series of texts describing famine and other troubles have been correctly assigned to this point in time. Deriving from the necropolis of Deir el-Bersha and the nearby alabaster quarries of Hatnub, they were inscribed under the gubernatorial authority of the nomarchs of the important 'Hare'-nome.

In any case, the father of Ammenemes I was one Senwosret, who appears in a number of later contexts with the title of 'God's Father', generally used to distinguish the non-royal parent of a king and, on occasion, the father of a queen. His mother was named Neferet.

With the accession of Ammenemes I, founder of the Twelfth Dynasty, the Middle Kingdom, inaugurated by the reunification of Egypt under Montjuhotpe II, got fully underway. In spite of the fact that the latter king was remembered for the feat into the New Kingdom, official propaganda rapidly cast Ammenemes in the role of the true unifier. A number of 'prophesies' became current, in particular one put into the mouth of a certain Neferti, at the court of Seneferu, back in the Fourth Dynasty; after relating how the land had been turned 'topsy-turvy' (see p.44, above), the prophet declares:

> Then a king will come from the south,
> Ameny [Amenemhat/Ammenemes] his name,
> Son of a woman of Nubia, a child of Upper Egypt,
> He will take the White Crown,
> He will wear the Red Crown ....
> Rejoice, O people of this time,
> For this son of man will make his name for ever:
> The evil-minded, the treasonous,
> They will fall silent for fear of him.
> Asiatics will fall to his sword,

Libyans will fall to his flame ....
One will build the Walls-of-the-Ruler,
To bar the Asiatics from entering Egypt.
They will beg for water ...,
Then order will return to its place ....

A key act of the new king was to transfer the royal seat from Thebes, the royal city of the Inyotefs and Montjuhotpes, to a new site in the north. While Ammenemes was a southerner, with possibly Nubian blood in his veins, rule of the Delta was difficult from so far up-stream, as was the defence of the north-east and north-western frontiers: the 'Walls-of-the-Ruler' referred to by Neferti were a series of forts intended to protect the area north of Suez. Accordingly, the city of Itj-tawy, 'Seizer of the Two Lands', was established in the area of modern Lisht, to remain the main residence of Pharaoh for the next four hundred years.

There had certainly been some reordering of the nomarchies in the wake of Montjuhotpe II's reunification, with the former Herakleopolitan-loyalist families replaced by those more favourable to the new regime. However, the nomes remained the principal building-blocks of the state, although now regulated so as to avoid any repeat of the aggrandizement and fighting of the First Inter-mediate Period. Amongst the best-known of the provincial rulers are those of the Oryx Nome, buried in a series of beautiful tomb-chapels at Beni Hasan. One of the scions of the line, Khnum-hotpe I, accompanied Ammenemes I on a cruise down the Nile with a flotilla of twenty ships, intended to stamp royal authority on any who might contemplate opposition to the regime.

In the king's twentieth regnal year, he appointed his son, Sesostris I, as his co-regent. In view of his high office prior to accession, Ammenemes was doubtless growing old, and required the aid of his son in carrying out some of the more active aspects of kingship. Amongst these were the leadership of military expeditions, in particular into Nubia, whose full return to Egyptian control was now contemplated. Other warlike activities extended into the Sinai and the Western Desert, and it was while King Sesostris was returning from a campaign against the Libyans, ten years after his induction as co-regent, that Ammenemes I's life was abruptly ended. The king himself is made to relate what happened in a posthumous address to his son:

I took an hour of rest, after the evening meal when night had come. I lay on my bed, for I was weary. As I began to fall asleep, weapons intended for my protection were turned against me, while I (dozed) like a snake in the desert. I awoke at the commotion, and found that it was an attack by the bodyguard. Had I been able to seize weapons, I would have made the cowards flee; but no one is strong at night; no one can fight alone; no success is possible without a helper.

So blood was shed while I was without you; before the courtiers had heard that I handed over to you; before I had sat down to talk with you. For I had not been prepared for it, I had not thought of it, had not foreseen the failing of servants ....

So died the king at the hands of assassins. Out on the margins of the desert, a messenger came to Sesostris who, fearing further treachery, sped back to Itj-tawy without informing his staff, to secure his throne. Other princes in the expedition may have been implicated in the plot, for an overheard discussion involving one of them was the pretext for the flight of one Sinuhe, the basis of one of the great works of Egyptian literature, *The Story of Sinuhe*.

Nevertheless, Sesostris I succeeded in preventing further insurrection, and interred his father in his pyramid at Lisht, a monument perhaps begun fairly late in the reign. This seems to have replaced an earlier monument at Thebes that was apparently to have followed the form of that of Montjuhotpe II. Of a form echoing Old Kingdom practice, Ammenemes' ultimate funerary monument was surrounded by the sepulchres of his family and followers. The former included his wife Neferytatenen, mother of Sesostris I, and daughter, Neferusherit. King Ammenemes' burial chamber has never been entered in modern times, the room having been flooded by ground-water, and the pyramid is but a shapeless pile of rubble, a sad memorial to a great king.

Sesostris III

c. 1881-1840 BC

The years of the Twelfth Dynasty were those of great stability and development. The long reign of Sesostris I saw Nubia occupied down as far as Buhen, with a presence extended further south. Extensive building took place, including the core of the temple of Karnak, and various works at Heliopolis. Sesostris I's co-regent and successor, Ammenemes II had led a Nubian expedition while yet a prince, and more are recorded on the great annalistic inscription produced during his likewise-lengthy occupation of the throne.

The next king, Sesostris II, is less well-attested, but seems to have been responsible for the large-scale development of the Fayoum, the 'oasis' region, some 70 kilometres south of modern Cairo. There he built his pyramid, the first of its kind to be constructed from brick, rather than stone, a technique which was continued by his successors. He was followed by his son, Sesostris III, who was to become a most distinguished occupant of the Egyptian throne, and worshipped as a god for many centuries after his death.

Material dating to his reign is found at a number of locations, particularly in the southern part of Egypt. The king's statues are notable for their extremely naturalistic treatment of the features: rather than the idealism of earlier works, they give every indication of being true portraits. The heavy eye-lids and lined countenance are particularly distinctive, making the face of Sesostris III one of the most easily-recognizable in Egyptian art. The later examples seem to show an increasing 'world-weariness', particularly where the image is carved in granite, the grain of the stone deepening the impression. Such a departure from previous artistic conventions is clearly of ideological significance, and when combined with the epithets used for the king in contemporary texts, we seem to see a considered attempt to present the king as possessing a 'concerned, serious and thoughtful' outlook upon his great office.

The reign of Sesostris III is the last in which one finds widespread examples of the monuments of the nomarchs of the various provinces. It was long believed that this reflected a conscious 'breaking' of the power of the nomarchs, but it now seems more likely that it was the indirect result of an increasing centralisation of the administration, leading to a gradual withering away of the great local 'courts', as their leaders moved to work for the king at the national capital.

Fig. 19. King Sesostris III: a granite statue from the temple of Montju-hotpe II at Deir el-Bahari.

There is relatively little evidence for Egyptian military activity in the direction of Palestine during the Middle Kingdom. That there was concern about elements from that direction is indicated by the inclusion of the names of various rulers and cities in a set of so-called 'Execration Texts'. These were lists of malevolent elements, written on pottery vessels and figures, and then smashed to symbolically disable them. That practical action was sometimes taken against the Asiatic 'foes' is shown by the expedition mounted by Sesostris III which reached some considerable distance beyond the later site of Jerusalem. Sobkkhu, to whose stela we owe our knowledge of the operation, records his pride at his capture of an enemy soldier.

The same man was also involved in Sesostris III's expeditions into Nubia, which were far more extensive, and marked the full subjugation of the territory by the Egyptian crown. The first campaign of which we are aware came about in year 8; in preparation for this, the king had earlier undertaken the (re)construction of a canal just south of Aswan, perhaps originally cut back in the days of Nemtyemsaf I. The rapids of the First

60

Cataract were always a major hinderance to southward-bound shipping, and the existence of a navigable channel made the passage of men and equipment far easier. Thus, Sesostris was able to lead his fleet through the new waterway bound for Kush, with the intention of establishing a proper southern boundary for Egypt, and regulating its intercourse with the peoples who lived south of it.

This was set at Semna, where a whole complex of forts were built or rebuilt to house Egyptian governors and garrisons. These massive constructions, now lost below the waters of Lake Nasser, incorporated huge bastions and other defences, and contained a great complex of military and civil structures. These included very large grain-stores, most probably intended to provide supplies for campaigning soldiery temporarily camped in the area, rather than the permanent personnel.

The stela erected at the boundary makes clear the king's intentions regarding the relationship between his Egyptian-Nubia and the territory lying to the south:

> Southern boundary, made in year 8, under the person of King Sesostris III ..., to prevent any Nubian crossing it by water or by land, with a ship or any Nubian herds, except for any Nubian who shall come to trade at Mirgissa, or with a commission. Every good thing will be done for them, without allowing a Nubian ship to pass Semna, going downstream – ever!

Further campaigning is recorded for years 10, 16 and 19, the king's penultimate visit to Nubia resulting in the erection of a second boundary stela at Semna, together with a duplicate at another fort, Uronarti, part of which expresses the contempt which the Egyptians felt for their southern neighbours:

> I have established my boundary further south than my fathers,
> I have added to what was given to me.
> I am a king who speaks and (then) does,
> What my heart plans is done by my arm ....
> A coward is he who is driven back from his border,
> Since the Nubian listens, to fall at a word:
> To answer him is to make him retreat;
> Attack him: he will turn his back;
> Retreat: he will start attacking.

They are not people worthy of respect,
They are wretches, craven-hearted!
My person has seen it: it is not a lie!

The stela concludes with a passage that well illustrates the pride that Sesostris III felt for his achievements in the south, and his heartfelt wish that none would undo his efforts:

> As for any son of mine who shall maintain this border that my person has made: he is my son, born of my person. A true son is he who is the champion of his father, who guards the border of his begetter. But, as for he who abandons it, who fails to fight for it: he is not my son, he is not born of me!
> Now, see, my person has had an image made of my person at this border which my person has made, in order that you might maintain it, in order that you might fight for it.

Although setting the frontier at Semna, at the Second Cataract, the Egyptians regularly penetrated into the territory beyond, Sesostris III's southernmost attestation being a record of the height of the inundation at Dal, many kilometres beyond Semna, in year 10. The intervening area cannot have been of much interest to the king, apart from a strategic point of view; it was a most inhospitable land, made clear by its modern name, the *Batn el-Hajar*, the 'Belly of Rocks'.

For his tomb, Sesostris III did not follow his father in being buried in the Fayoum, but returned to Dahshur, the necropolis of Seneferu of the Old Kingdom, and also Ammenemes II. There he built his now-severely mutilated brick pyramid, devoid of all moveable funerary equipment when entered by archaeologists in the 1890s. The complex is interesting in being essentially a copy of the enclosure of Djoser's now-ancient Step Pyramid, and thus wholly unlike those of his predecessors. To cement the link with the past, a pair of sarcophagi were extracted from below the Third Dynasty monument, and interred at the north end of the *temenos*. Other shafts and galleries contained the bodies of Sesostris III's family, including his wife, Neferhenut. A considerable amount of jewellery survived near the sarcophagi of a number of the king's daughters, and now graces the Cairo Museum; more was found within the complex during the winter of 1994/5.

Fig. 20. The 'Fish-offerers' double statue, probably representing Sesostris III and Ammenemes III wearing a primitive priestly costume. The piece was later usurped by Psusennes I at Tanis.

In addition to his pyramid, the king built a cenotaph at Abydos, comprising a series of chapels, dummy mastabas, and an extraordinarily complex underground tomb. This incorporated all kinds of devices to mislead potential robbers, in spite of being only a dummy. Inevitably, the plunderers ultimately succeeded in locating the sarcophagus and robbed it of whatever it had once contained.

The posthumous cult of Sesostris III was particularly strong in Nubia. At the fortress-towns he had founded around the Second Cataract, temples were dedicated to him during the New Kingdom, and in later times his fame merged with that of other warrior-kings to produce the world-conquering hero 'Sesostris' of the Classical writers. According to Herodotus, he sailed into the Indian Ocean, and then marched through the Levant into Europe, defeating the Scythians and Thracians before halting. Regrettably, there is no evidence that any Egyptian king ever got this far, although Herodotus records that he himself saw examples of the 'columns' (stelae?) that he was told marked the progress of Sesostris. Nevertheless, excavation continues to produce the un-expected, and it is not beyond the bounds of possibility that some fragment may yet emerge that will shed some light on real events that lay behind the legend.

Ammenemes III

c. 1842-1794 BC

The eldest son of Sesostris III was Ammenemes III; he would appear to have served as co-regent for a considerable period before the elder king's death. From this phase appear to date a series of dual sculptures showing the naturalistic features that are to be seen on images of both kings. These pieces are of unusual types, a statue showing the monarchs dressed in archaic priestly dress and offering fish (fig. 20). A whole set of sphinxes reduce human elements to a minimum and for many years were wrongly attrib-uted to the Palestinian Hyksos rulers who were to dominate the north of Egypt a hundred and fifty years later. Later rulers approp-riated all these pieces, slicing the sphinxes into two separate figures, and reinscribing them.

Unlike his father, Ammenemes III has left us few memorials of military activities. Nevertheless, the wide distribution of his memorials makes it clear that he was, in the terms of Sesos-tris III's Nubian stelae, a 'true son ... who is the champion of his father'. Reforms in the national administration were continued, the country now being divided into three administrative regions, controlled by departments based at the national capital. These oversaw the activities of subordinate local officials, who no longer possessed the extensive devolved power with which they had previously been endowed.

An area of the country close to Ammenemes III's heart was the Fayoum, the land surrounding the large lake, the Birket Qarun that lies to the west of the Nile, fed by the Bahr Yousef, a channel that diverges from the main river north of Asyut. The region had received the attention of Sesostris II, as is shown by the construction of his pyramid there, at Lahun, but it was only under his grandson that more extensive works were carried out there – although not the actual *digging* of the lake, as was claimed by Herodotus! In particular, a barrage was constructed to regulate the flow of the water into the lake, thus reclaiming a large fertile area, which was then protected by an earthen embankment. To mark his contribution, Ammenemes III erected two colossal statues at Biyahmu, standing upon high bases, overlooking the lake. He also carried out building work at a number of the local sanctuaries, including the temple of Medinet Maadi.

Ammenemes III worked extensively the turquoise mines of the Sinai, greatly enlarging the temple of Serabit el-Khadim, which existed solely as a result of the pharaohs' regular exploitation of the areas' resources. Other regions which saw Egyptian expeditions bent on the extraction of raw materials were the Wadi Hammamat and the diorite quarries of the Nubian desert.

The king's principal wife was named Aat. She was buried in a chamber in the pyramid that Ammenemes III began at Dahshur; this arrangement is most unusual, all other pyramids being built with only the king's interment in mind. However, while still under construction, the pyramid suffered a major structural failure. As had happened nearly a thousand years before, only a short distance away at Seneferu's Bent Pyramid, massive cracks opened in roofing blocks, leading, after attempted repairs, to the abandonment of the pyramid as the king's burial place: later, it would be used for the interment of a number of female members of the royal family.

For a fresh tomb, the king turned to the Fayoum, building a new brick pyramid at Hawara, overlooking the barrage that was the key to the province's prosperity. There he was at length .

Fig. 21. King Ammenemes III, from Hawara.

interred, his burial chamber having been briefly used to contain the burial of his daughter, Neferuptah, before her reburial in a small pyramid some kilometres to the south. There is some evidence to suggest that Neferuptah may have been regarded as the king's potential successor, in the absence of any surviving son, but was denied the chance of becoming a female pharaoh by her own premature demise. Ammenemes III's Hawara pyramid has one of the most elaborate substructures of any such sepulchre, with at its core a burial chamber carved from a single block of quartzite, the hardest stone worked by ancient man.

In his final few years, Ammenemes III seems to have shared his throne with his nominated successor, Ammenemes IV, who may have been of non-royal birth. The latter's independent reign was, however, short, the king being succeeded by Ammenemes III's daughter, Sobkneferu, the second known female king in Egyptian history and fulfilling the frustrated destiny of her elder sister. With her passing, the Twelfth Dynasty came to a sudden end, being followed by a line whose relationships are distinctly confused.

Neferhotpe I and Sobkhotpe IV

c. 1720-1700 BC

The transition between the Twelfth Dynasty and the Thirteenth seems to have been peaceful enough, but the contrast between the two is striking: in place of well-documented reigns of substantial lengths, we have a huge number of kings with brief tenures of the throne, and of such obscurity that the exact order of many of them is unknown.

The dynasty seems to open with a king named Sobkhotpe I, He set the pattern for many of his successors by ruling for no more than three years. He also began a pattern by including the name of his father, one Amenemhat, in his nomen cartouche; on this basis, it is not unlikely that he was a son of Ammenemes IV. Similarly, the second ruler of the dynasty, Sonbef, may also have been Ammenemes' son.

The unfinished remains of a number of the tombs of the kings of the Thirteenth Dynasty lie at South Saqqara and Dahshur. Their pyramidal superstructures were of brick, overlying substructures whose complexity increased with every generation in an attempt to outwit the inevitable tomb robbers. While the pyramid remained the ideal, certain kings had to resort to simple shaft-burials, either through poverty or lack of time. One such sepulchre has been identified alongside the Dahshur pyramid of Ammenemes III, belonging to King Hor. Ironically, he benefitted from his grave's insignificance, since it was only partially robbed in antiquity, thus revealing to us the kind of equipment that accompanied a Middle Kingdom monarch to the afterlife.

The Thirteenth Dynasty being replete with short-lived kings, it was long felt that the real power was usually in the hands of a series of closely-related viziers, the actual pharaohs being little more than figureheads. More recent work has cast doubt on this interpretation, and it is unclear how far, if at all, matters diverged from normal Egyptian governmental practice.

Although much is obscure about the dynasty, one thing that is clear is that it did not comprise a single family line, there being a number of monarchs who were undoubtedly born commoners. Interestingly, these include some of those who are the most prominent of the period. Firstly, there is Sobkhotpe III, the off-spring of one Montjuhotpe and the lady Iuhetibu. His predecessors had all been short-lived, with certain clues pointing to disorder, or even military insurrection. In particular, one of them had taken the nomen 'Imyromesha' ('the General') and followed a ruler, Khendjer, who had both suffered the erasure of his names from certain monuments, and may have been denied burial in his own pyramid. This evidence is certainly suggestive of an irregular succession in this case, at least.

In contrast to many of these preceding kings, Sobkhotpe III is fairly well attested, particularly by his work at Medamud. He is known to have sired two daughters, but there is no record of any sons. While he had at least two brothers, who were granted the title of 'king's son', he was actually followed on the throne by an apparently unrelated man, one Neferhotpe, son of Haankhef (A) and Kem. There is no sign of royal blood in the family, the new king's paternal grandfather, Nehi, also being a commoner.

A number of places preserve traces of Neferhotpe I's activities, from Byblos in the Lebanon to Buhen in Nubia. These foreign attestations suggest that Egyptian influence was still in place in some of its old spheres. From Egypt itself come monuments at Karnak and in the area of the First Cataract. Particularly interesting are Neferhotpe's memorials from Abydos. The Thirteenth Dynasty had considerable interest in the holy city, and on a sandstone stela the king records how he came to Abydos to re-establish the proper form of the image and rituals of the god Osiris. Before doing so, he arranged that extensive researches be made in the archives of the temple of Atum at Heliopolis to dis-cover the original specifications, which had presumably been disregarded in recent years.

Also at Abydos, Neferhotpe I appropriated one, if not all four, of a set of stelae that had been erected by a predecessor, whose name has been read both as that of King Wegaf, and as that of King Seth(y), both of whom had ruled only a few years earlier. These stelae had been intended to mark out the sacred area at Abydos leading up to the Archaic necropolis at Umm el-Qaab, by then regarded as containing the tomb of the mortuary god, Osiris. Another king, whose name has been erased but may be that of King Khendjer, had also adorned the tomb of Horus Djer, believed to be that of the deity himself, with the fine recumbent image that is now in Cairo (cf. p.16, above).

Neferhotpe's usurpation was presumably part of his attempt to regularise the activities surrounding the cult of Osiris and his associate deities. Thus he doubtless re-enacted the earlier king's decree that anyone trespassing on the marked-out area (alive, or dead, by having a tomb built there) would be burnt. This sacred area seems to have been the wadi leading up to Umm el-Qaab from the area of the Osiris temple, the scene of the great procession that was the highlight of the god's 'mystery play', doubtless an event with which the king's visit was intended to coincide.

Neferhotpe I's reign seems to have lasted some eleven years. His pyramid is as yet unidentified, and by the time he died he had probably outlived his son, Haankhaf (B). Accordingly, he was succeeded by his younger brother, Sihathor, whose reign was to be brief. On his demise, a third son of Haankhaf A took the throne – Sobkhotpe IV.

A long inscription from Karnak tells us much about the administration of the south, in addition confirming that the national capital remained at Itj-tawy. That Egypt still maintained an interest in Nubia, heeding Sesostris III's monumental exhortations, is shown by the fact that Sobkhotpe IV fought there. Nevertheless, as we shall see, not long afterwards Nubia would become an independent power, and prepared to ally against her former overlords.

A whole series of the king's officials are known by name. The vizier was Iymeru Neferkare, apparently not related to the family that had held the office down to the reign of the third Sobkhotpe. Of importance was the great steward, Nebankh, who had important family links with the royal family, his niece, Nubkhaes, ultimately marrying one of Sobkhotpe IV's immediate successors.

Sobkhotpe IV is attested by monuments at sites throughout Egypt, in both the Delta and in Upper Egypt. Nevertheless, it was possibly in his reign that the first signs of the disintegration of the Egyptian state appeared, the Greek writer, Artapanos, reporting that in the reign of 'Chenephres' (= Khaneferre?) Egypt was divided into a number of kingdoms. While without direct corroboration, the context of the breakup of the kingdom a few decades later would suggest initial moves around this time.

Having occupied the throne for something approaching a decade, the king was succeeded by his son, Sobkhotpe, who thus became the fifth ruler of the name. Sobkhotpe IV's tomb has also not yet been excavated, but most probably lay in the Saqqara/ Dahshur area, where a number of pyramids of this date still await examination.

The last fifty years of the Thirteenth Dynasty seem to represent a gradual decline. Although featuring some of the dynasty's longest reigns, a withdrawal from Levantine and Nubian commitments was accompanied by the establishment of a whole new state in Upper Nubia, and the consolidation of the control of the north-east Delta under a line of Palestinian rulers, based on the site of Tell el-Daba. Ultimately, however, the latter were in turn displaced by a new group of Asiatics, who would pursue a far more aggressive policy that would soon engulf the whole of northern Egypt. This group is known to history as the Hyksos.

VIII   The Liberators

Taa II

c. 1558-1553 BC

Around 1650 BC, the rule of northern Egypt passed from the
Thirteenth Dynasty, the heirs of the house of Ammenemes, to the
Hyksos, a group of princes of Palestinian origin. They exercised
their control from the city of Avaris (Tell el-Daba) in the eastern
Nile delta, a place gradually settled by Levantines since the
middle of the Twelfth Dynasty. Having apparently displaced the
previous elite, they rapidly extended their dominion and ruled
there with full pharaonic titles for something over a century. Their
city displayed many aspects of Palestinian culture, as well as
many monuments looted from the Memphite and Fayoum regions.
These items included sculptures of Middle Kingdom kings (eg. that
shown in fig. 20), and even the cap-stone from the now-lost
pyramid of King Aya.

At the same time, or some time earlier, perhaps soon after
Sobkhotpe IV's campaign, Egypt's Nubian province became de-
coupled from the state, a line of native rulers setting up their own
kingdom, based on the town of Kerma. Their remains show an
interesting mix of indigenous traditions and Egyptian survivals,
the former being very clearly visible in the royal tombs at Kerma,
huge tumuli, under which the king lay on a bed, surrounded by the
bodies of his sacrificed servants.

The rump of the old Egyptian regime fled southwards to the
ancestral city of Thebes, where they initially established what is
now known as the Sixteenth Dynasty. Ruled by kings bearing such
time-honoured Theban names as Inyotef and Montjuhotpe, they
seem to have initially co-existed with their northern neighbours.
However, in the time of the Hyksos Khyan, the Palestinians

pushed south and for a time ruled the whole of the Nile valley down to at least Gebelein, if not the Nubian frontier.

This may have represented over-extension by the northerners, since Theban independence was soon reasserted in the form of the Seventeenth Dynasty. Some form of accommodation would appear to have then been reached between the two regimes, perhaps with Thebes accepting the Hyksos' nominal overlordship for a period of time. However, this was to change in the reign of the penultimate monarch of the dynasty, Taa II. His mother was Tetisherit, the daughter of the judge, Tjenna, and the Lady Neferu; although the monuments nowhere state it, his father was presumably his predecessor, Taa I. The king married his sister, Ahhotpe, who bore him a number of children.

Our knowledge of the quarrel which broke out between Thebes and Avaris is derived from a later folk tale, which tells of a complaint by the Hyksos King Apophis that the hippopotami of Thebes were disturbing his sleep. The origins of this obviously trumped-up charge are clearly in some way mythological; of the war which clearly followed we know little, apart from a fundamental part of its outcome:

Amongst the surviving royal mummies is that of King Taa II, surnamed Qen, 'the brave'. It is poorly preserved, largely disarticulated, with only part of the skin preserved, but it is the state of the head which grips one's attention. The skull is covered with horrific wounds: a dagger thrust behind the ear may have felled the king, after which weapons rained down upon him. Mace-blows smashed his cheek and nose, while a battle-axe cut through the bone above his forehead. The mummy's mouth remains with its lips drawn back in the king's final anguish.

Although some have suggested that the king fell at the hands of assassins, the sheer violence and variety of weapons argues far more clearly for death on the battlefield. What is more, the Palestinian origin of the battle axe that crushed the kings skull has been proven by careful comparisons of the wound with actual examples of contemporary weapons of this type.

Taa II was buried below a small pyramid at Dira Abu'l-Naga in the Theban necropolis, his mummy being removed to a communal place of safety at Deir el-Bahari during the Twenty-first Dynasty. The body came to rest in the Cairo Museum in 1881.

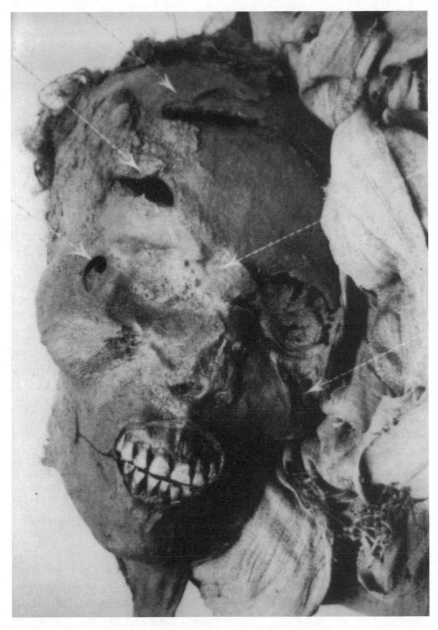

Fig. 22. The head of the mummy of King Taa II, showing the horrific wounds that caused his death.

Kamose

c. 1553-1549 BC

Kamose' relationship to Taa II is uncertain: it is generally thought that he was his elder son, although, it has also been suggested that Kamose may have been a younger brother of Taa. The identity of his queen is likewise unclear, but may have been Ahmose-Meryetamun, in which case she was his sister.

Our knowledge of the events of Kamose's reign is derived from the two stelae that he set up in the temple of Karnak. These tell that in his third year he decided to resume hostilities against the Hyksos, which seem to have been discontinued following the death of Taa II, leaving the Thebans in control of only the section of Egypt between Ashmunein in Middle Egypt and Aswan. As the king himself put it:

> To what end is my strength, when a chieftain is in Avaris, and another in Kush, and I sit together with an Asiatic and an African, each man holding his slice of this Egypt?

Accordingly, Kamose sent his forces northwards, fighting his way through the country until, at length, he reached a point deep inside Hyksos territory, 80 kilometres south of the Fayoum at Sheikh Fadl. During this exercise, a Hyksos royal messenger was captured, carrying a letter from King Apophis to his ally, the king of Nubia, calling upon him to come to his aid, by attacking the Egyptians from the south while their main forces were engaged in the Delta. It is evident that Kamose had not previously feared assault from that direction. Thus warned, he was able to take steps to protect himself against such an eventuality. Indeed, there is evidence to suggest that as part of this, Kamose launched a southern offensive, conceivably as far as Buhen.

Although he had pushed the Hyksos back from the Theban heartland, it appears that Kamose died before the next northern campaigning-season. He was buried in his small West Theban pyramid, the body later being removed and reinterred in rubble around 700 metres away. Regrettably, the mummy collapsed into a mass of bones and dust on discovery: thus we know nothing of the cause of the king's death.

Amosis

c. 1549-1524 BC

Amosis, son of Taa II and Ahhotpe, seems to have been but a boy on Kamose's death, and it would appear that no attempt to complete his predecessor's work was made during the first decade of the reign. Ultimately, however, operations began once again, the Thebans managing to launch an attack on Heliopolis before pressing on into the Delta to finally settle scores with the Hyksos in Avaris.

The assaults against Avaris are recounted in the auto-biography of Ahmose, son of Ibana, a naval officer from El-Kab. The siege was fairly drawn out, interrupted by the need to put down insurrections in already-liberated territory; it was finally being completed somewhere between regnal years 12 and 15. This was followed up by a six-year siege of the south-west Palestinian fortress of Sharuhen, whose surrender marked the formal expulsion of the Hyksos. This great victory was accompanied by the decoration of deserving personnel, Ahmose receiving the 'Gold of Bravery', along with captives as slaves.

The Hyksos capital then became an Egyptian royal residence, and from this period come some intriguing remains. A large palace-building revealed many fragments of fresco-painting that were clearly in the style of Minoan Crete. No other Cretan artifacts were to be found, but the most likely explanation may be that Amosis concluded a diplomatic marriage with the Aegean kingdom, and that the lady had a residence here, decorated for her by artists from her homeland.

Having freed Egypt of foreign rule, Amosis then turned his attention to Nubia. Kamose may have managed to regain at least some of the area; now, Egyptian forces reasserted rule over the area south of the Second Cataract, enabling the establishment of a new civil administration, headed by a Viceroy, the first of whom under Amosis may have been one Djehuty.

The king's absence in Nubia may have encouraged rebellions by former Hyksos-allies in Middle Egypt. In particular, one Teti-en is named, conceivably the same man who had been a foe of Kamose over a decade earlier. This period of uprisings seems to have brought the queen-mother, Ahhotpe, to the fore, a stela praising her for being 'one who cares for Egypt ... (who) has pacified Upper Egypt and expelled her rebels'. It was perhaps for her role in these events that she received the gold flies, known to be awards for valour, that were found on her mummy.

Having resolved matters within Egypt and the 'near-abroad', Amosis seems to have returned to Palestine to undertake a further campaign to extend the area of Egyptian power into Asia. It is possible that his advance may have pushed as far as the Euphrates, on the basis of an allusion in a stela of Tuthmosis I. Thus, by the end of his reign, Amosis had expunged the shame of Hyksos domination, restored Egypt's imperium on the upper Nile, and laid the foundation for his successors' expansion into Syria-Palestine and beyond.

Like his father, Amosis married his sister: Ahmose-Nefertiri. They had a number of children, including Amosis' original heir, Amosis-ankh, his eventual successor, Amenophis I, the latter's wife, Meryetamun, the Princes Ahmose-Sipairi, Siamun and Ramose(?) and the Princess Sitamun.

The king's tomb remains unknown, but his body was found in the Third Intermediate Period cache of royal mummies at Deir el-Bahari. Like Sesostris III, he also had a cenotaph at South Abydos, comprising a cliff temple, far out into the desert, a dummy tomb, and a pyramid and temple on the edge of the cultivation. The pyramid, nearly 70 metres square, is the last known royal example to be built in Egypt-proper. Excavations since 1993 have revealed that the pyramid-temple had been decorated with battle-scenes that may depict the expulsion of the Hyksos, including the earliest known Egyptian representation of horses.

IX   The Queen and the Conqueror

Tuthmosis III and Hatshepsut

c. 1479-1424 BC

Amenophis I's reign appears to have been fairly uneventful, without any further known action in Asia. He consolidated the achievements of Amosis and undertook a considerable amount of building work. Later he was regarded as patron god of the Theban necropolis, alongside his mother, Ahmose-Nefertiri, whose posthumous renown exceeded his own. Apparently childless, Amenophis I was succeeded by a man of uncertain antecedents, Tuthmosis I. It is highly probable that the latter may have been a member of the royal family, quite possibly a grandson of Amosis. It has been suggested that Tuthmosis' father was Prince Ahmose-Sipairi, who has a prominence on the monuments that seems far higher than one would have expected for a royal son who never ruled. However, the matter remains uncertain.

Tuthmosis I was a warrior, and undertook extensive campaigns in Nubia and Syria, reaching at least as far as Amosis had done. He also built extensively, adding two pylons and a pair of obelisks to the temple of Karnak, not to mention constructions elsewhere. By his principal wife, Ahmose, who was either his own sister, or that of Amenophis I, Tuthmosis had at least one daughter, and probably also his elder sons, Amenmose and Wadjmose. The former seems to have been born long before the king's accession, held the title of Generalissimo and erected a monument near the Great Sphinx at Giza and was heir to the throne before dying prematurely.

A further son was borne by another spouse, Mutneferu, who was to succeed his father as Tuthmosis II. His half-sister, Hatshepsut, became his consort. Apart from a police action into Nubia, little is known of his reign of around a decade. By Hatshepsut, he fathered two daughters, Neferure and Neferubity, but no sons; his only known male offspring was born to a lesser wife, Iset, and named Thutmose (Tuthmosis) after his father and grandfather.

While still young, the prince underwent priestly training in the great temple of Amun at Karnak, and it was there that he appears to have been formally proclaimed heir to the throne by Tuthmosis II. His accession to the throne came sooner than might have been expected: on Tuthmosis II's death a short while later, he became king as Tuthmosis III. As the new king was no more than a child, his aunt, Hatshepsut, became regent and ruled Egypt in his name.

The elevation of a queen-dowager to such a position was by no means unusual, with possible earlier examples going back to Meryetneith in the First Dynasty. However, from the first, Hatshepsut appears more prominent than one would have expected. She appeared on temple walls, for example at Semna in the Sudan, as well as on stelae; for her tomb she had commissioned a fine quartzite sarcophagus of a type only adopted a year or two earlier as a prerogative of kings. Her dominance is expressed in the Theban tomb-autobiography of the official, Ineni, as follows:

> [Tuthmosis II] went forth to heaven ...; his son stood in his place as king of the Two Lands, having become ruler upon the seat of his begetter. His sister (i.e. female relative), the divine wife, Hatshepsut, settled the affairs of the Two Lands according to her own plans. Egypt was made to labour with bowed head for her, the excellent seed of the god, who came forth from him.

Nevertheless, for the first seven years of the young Tuthmosis' reign, Hatshepsut displayed no more than queenly attributes – the traditional vulture headdress, and the titles of King's Great Wife and God's Wife. A dramatic change occurred, however, in year 7 of Tuthmosis III's reign. Perhaps prompted by the king's impending majority, Hatshepsut had herself proclaimed 'king' – the Egyptian title we translate as queen means no more than 'king's wife'. As such, she almost invariably had herself represented in male garb, with full pharaonic titulary, which only occasionally gave away her sex by dropping in the feminine grammatical ending, 't'.

Fig. 23. The co-rulers, Hatshepsut and Tuthmosis III, depicted on the Red Chapel, a quartzite shrine erected by the queen at Karnak.

As king, she did nothing to diminish the nominal status of Tuthmosis III; she dated her rule by his regnal years, and represented him frequently upon her monuments: on the surface, at least, she posed as a normal co-regent. She did, however, do much to assert her legitimacy, publishing a fiction by which her father, Tuthmosis I, had actually elevated her to the kingship while he yet lived. In support of this, she recounts her birth as being in traditional pharaonic style, with her mother impregnated by Amun-Re himself, disguised as the king, and attended at her confinement by Amun, the god Khnum, who had fashioned the divine baby on his potter's wheel, and the frog-goddess Heqet.

The fourteen years during which Hatshepsut and Tuthmosis III shared the throne seem to have seen a division of labour, with the king responsible for military matters, and the queen-regnant for home affairs, together with more peaceful foreign endeavours. As his contribution to the former, Tuthmosis seems to have led at least two campaigns into Palestine, and another pair into Nubia. For her part, Hatshepsut's best known foreign activity is the trading expedition to Punt, the Red Sea state which had been a trading partner of Egypt since at least the time of Sahure. Amongst items brought back were myrrh trees, sacks of myrrh, ivory, woods, apes and other exotic items. This voyage is recorded on the walls of the fine funerary temple which Hatshepsut had built at Deir el-Bahari, next to that of the Eleventh Dynasty king, Montjuhotpe II.

Hatshepsut's funerary temple formed one of the two elements of the typical mortuary installation of a New Kingdom monarch. From the Old Kingdom down to the beginning of the Eighteenth Dynasty, kings had almost invariably aspired to a pyramid, whether large or small, depending on their resources or life-span. The body had been interred below it, with a chapel adjoining to provide for the needs of the spirit. From the reign of Tuthmosis I, if not any earlier, this scheme had been replaced by one which separated the elements. The pyramid itself disappeared, unless the pyramidal peak, El-Qurn, which towers above the Theban necropolis, was regarded as a substitute. The subterranean chambers were transferred to a desert wadi behind the screen of cliffs that front the city of the dead: today, this is known to the world as the Valley of the Kings.

The final element was the chapel, which was placed in front of the cliffs, on the low desert overlooking the fields. They follow the general pattern of contemporary temples, with certain special elements specific to their role in the royal funerary cult. Hatshepsut's follows its Middle Kingdom neighbour and certain other temples in being built in terraces against the mountainside. The architect of this superb structure seems to have been one Senenmut; apparently a man of inconsequential birth, he rapidly rose in Hatshepsut's favour, becoming the tutor to her daughter, Neferure. A huge tomb-chapel was built for him on the Theban hills, with his separate burial chamber set just within the precincts of the queen's temple; this sepulchre was intended to contain a sarcophagus clearly made as a pair to Hatshepsut's own. Such is his prominence and intimacy with the queen, extending still further to the carving of his image inside the very shrines of her temple, that one does not seem rash in suggesting that their relationship was rather more than mere queen and courtier.

An interesting account of the queen's home policy is given in the Speos Artemidos, a rock chapel at Beni Hasan. It describes its construction and her systematic restoration of temples allegedly ruined as a result of the Hyksos interlude, brought to an end over eighty years previously. Part of her building programme is described in detail at Deir el-Bahari, where we are able to see and

Fig. 24. The mortuary temple Hatshepsut at Deir el-Bahari.

81

read of the quarrying and transport of two pairs of great granite obelisks, from the quarries at Aswan to Amun's temple at Karnak; a further relief from Karnak seems to record the erection there of the second, a work which was completed in year 16, possibly as part of jubilee celebrations. There are, however, some doubts as to whether this festival actually took place, as such festivities were normally only held after thirty years on the throne. On the other hand it is possible that Hatshepsut may have been counting from her installation as Queen-Consort, back at the death of her father.

Other works carried out under Hatshepsut's rule included quarrying of turquoise in the Sinai, and extensive construction work at Karnak, of which the obelisks were only part. Pylons were added, together with a new sanctuary and surrounding rooms, all in the finest style of the age.

Of Hatshepsut's two daughters, Neferubity seems to have died young. Her sister, Neferure, however, took over her mother's title of God's Wife on Hatshepsut's assumption of kingly status, possibly with the thought that she might one day actually succeed the queen on the throne: on one inscription, she appears to share the eleventh joint regnal year of Tuthmosis III and Hatshepsut. On the other hand, it is possible that Neferure may have married

Fig. 25. Hatshepsut's obelisks, from her Karnak Red Chapel.

82

her half-brother, Tuthmosis III, perhaps bearing his eldest son, Prince Amenemhat, not long afterwards.

Hatshepsut's reign came to an end twenty-two years after the death of her husband, Tuthmosis II. Nothing is known of her fate: as to whether she died in that year, or retired into private life, the monuments are silent. Then, two whole decades after her disappearance from the scene, a sudden assault was launched on her monuments by her erstwhile coregent. At Deir el-Bahari and elsewhere, the female king's names and images were erased from the walls of her temples and her statues removed and broken up. In some cases, her figures were replaced by those of her father, husband, or nephew; in others, the wall was left bearing the ghostly outline of Hatshepsut's former image. At Karnak, Hatshepsut's obelisks were surrounded by walls that hid her texts from public view.

Hatshepsut had taken over the tomb of her father, Tuthmosis I, in the Valley of the Kings, enlarging it, and placing her father's body in its new burial chamber, where she intended it to lie with hers in the fullness of time. For this reburial, she used a sarcophagus that she had made for herself soon after her assumption of kingly titles. She was now replacing it with a much larger and more splendid version, the old one being partially re-inscribed for the old king. After Hatshepsut's disappearance from the throne, Tuthmosis I's body was taken from the tomb altogether, and once again reburied, this time in a completely new tomb and sarcophagus, made for him by his grandson, Tuthmosis III. There seems, however, no reason to doubt that the female pharaoh was granted burial in her appropriated tomb.

The reason for the great delay in effacing Hatshepsut's memorials is difficult to fathom; had there been sufficient animosity between the coregents, surely Tuthmosis' attack on Hatshepsut's monuments would have occurred back in the twenties – rather than so very many years later. One possible explanation might be that Hatshepsut had indeed outlived year 22, and it was the eventual death of the ex-queen that prompted the mutilation of her monuments. For such an explanation, however, there is not one shred of hard evidence.

A further set of mysterious destructions of names and images concerns Senenmut, Hatshepsut's greatest intimate. Both his tomb and chapel have had names and figures erased, likewise Senenmut's reliefs in the Deir el-Bahari temple; his quartzite sarcophagus has been reduced to fragments, while a number of his numerous statues have had names erased and/or suffered some mutilation. It is usually stated that Senenmut's 'fall' was due to his losing the faith of his royal mistress – since the names of Hatshepsut are mostly intact on such items – or suffering at the hands of Tuthmosis III for siding with his aunt in their supposed 'feud'. However, there is no real evidence in favour of either of these scenarios: it is possible only to say that Senenmut suffered from the posthumous disfavour of persons unknown.

Although it appears that Tuthmosis III had undertaken military actions while reigning alongside Hatshepsut, it is following his re-accession to sole rule that we find extensive accounts of his campaigns, annual expeditions that were to cement his reputation as indisputably the greatest of all the warrior-pharaohs. The first of these began in year 22, when he left the north-eastern fortress of Tjel, bound for Gaza, with the intention of dealing with the threat to Egyptian power perceived as emanating from the ruler of Qadesh, a city-state on the Orontes. Having celebrated the twenty-third anniversary of his accession at Gaza, he pressed onwards to the town of Yehem, nearly 130 kilometres further on, where the army made camp.

While there, the king and his generals learned that the Prince of Qadesh had taken up residence at the city of Megiddo, just under 30 kilometres away, as the crow flies. There were three possible approaches to the enemy town, which lay on the other side of a hill. The advice of Tuthmosis' staff was that the Egyptians take one of the two longer, but easier, routes, which emerged from the hills around 13 kilometres north and south of Megiddo; this would, unfortunately, give the enemy ample warning of their approach. The king's view, however, was that they should risk taking the third route, leading directly over the hills to the city. The generals' view was that this was far too risky, the road being so narrow, only 9 metres wide at its most constricted, that there was the very real danger that the vanguard of the Egyptian army would have to join action before the rearguard had entered the pass. The king felt, however, that the risk was worth the possibility of surprising his foes, who would expect him to come by

Fig. 26. King Tuthmosis III smites his enemies (south face of the Seventh Pylon at Karnak).

one of the easier routes. Accordingly, the next morning, Tuthmosis III led his army into the hills, arriving above Megiddo at noon. It was, however, seven hours until the whole force had arrived, deploying to the north and south of the enemy town, before setting up camp with the intention of joining battle the next day.

The Egyptian attack seems to have achieved everything that the king intended, as the Qadeshi forces, encamped outside Megiddo rapidly broke and fled back towards the city walls. There, as the Egyptian account of the battle, carved on the walls of Karnak temple, records, the enemy 'abandoned their horses and gold and silver chariots, to enable them to be hauled up by their clothing into the town'. Unfortunately, the booty left behind by the retreating army proved too strong a temptation to the Egyptian troops, who lost valuable time in taking possession. Thus, the opportunity of capturing the enemy leaders while they were being dragged up the city walls, and storming the town in the confusion, was lost. Accordingly, it became necessary to dig in for a long siege, which was only successful after seven long months, and at the end of which the Prince of Qadesh managed to escape.

Three further cities of the Qadeshi alliance were also reduced during the campaign; mercy was shown to the defeated foes – a key feature of Tuthmosis III's strategy – new rulers being appointed from amongst their numbers, before the king returned to Egypt.

The next year's operation was a fairly simple march through Syria-Palestine, the army collecting gifts and tribute as it went, the same apparently being true of that of year 25. The latter, however, is interesting in providing the material for one of the most remarkable representations in an Egyptian temple, and providing a fascinating insight into Tuthmosis III's character. Rather than scenes of military might, we find row after row of representations of the flora and fauna of Palestine.

Year 29 saw the first campaign, of which records survive anyway, to press beyond the areas whose rule was confirmed by the Megiddo campaign; together with the next year's operation, it saw the king push up into Syria-proper, finally capturing the city of Qadesh itself. In his follow-up settlement, the sons of the defeated city-rulers were taken away to Egypt, both as hostages against their fathers' good behaviour, and also to educate an Egyptophile next-generation of rulers, to ease the perpetuation of an Egyptian hegemony.

The campaign of year 33 saw Tuthmosis III's crowning military achievement. Nearly fifty years before, his grandfather, Tuthmosis I, had reached the Euphrates, and left a commemorative stela there. Now, the third Tuthmosis crossed that great river-boundary, defeating in the process the king of Mitanni, one of the era's Great Powers, and erecting one of his own stelae next to Tuthmosis I's, together with another on the opposite side of the river. Having also pushed north to Carchemesh, Tuthmosis III had now extended Egyptian power to its greatest extent in Asia, and while in the area received gifts from not only the local rulers, but defeated Mitanni, and the kings of Babylon and the Hittites as well.

Campaigning continued in subsequent years; one cannot help suspecting that Tuthmosis III was at his happiest with his army, a number of whose generals are known. One, Amenemheb, has left an autobiography in his tomb which gives colour to a number of the events known from the formal annals. Another, Djehuty, is known from a later story, which tells of his seizure of the city of Joppa, through smuggling in troops, contained in baskets carried by donkeys.

Tuthmosis' last Asiatic campaign took place in year 42, once again fighting against his old foe, the ruler of Qadesh, whose city was now taken by storm. At its conclusion, perhaps perceiving that his fighting years were nearly over, the king commanded that the previous two decades' fighting be written-up on the walls of his new buildings at Karnak; these, incidentally, were to obliterate some of the works of Hatshepsut.

In Egypt and Nubia, Tuthmosis III was a great builder, large parts of the temple of Karnak being his work. One of the most interesting is his Festival Hall, its roof supported on columns imitating tent-poles. A number of obelisks were quarried, one of which, however, still remains joined to the bed-rock at Aswan, a fault having been found in it. Its intended partner was later erected at the back of Karnak by Tuthmosis IV; now it stands at St. John Lateran in Rome, the largest surviving obelisk.

Elsewhere, Western Thebes was host to his mortuary temple, and a new Deir el-Bahari sanctuary. Additionally, Medamud, Armant, Esna, Dendara, Kom Ombo and various Nubian sites are but examples of the places that benefitted from his construction work. Finely decorated tombs provide the names of many of his officials, in particular that of the vizier Rekhmire, whose chapel is both an artistic and cultural delight. Amongst its texts is one which comments on the king's skill in the hieroglyphic script, and another which comprises the king's traditional installation speech, in which he sets out the duties of his vizier, which he characterizes as 'bitter as gall'.

As already noted, the king's first wife may have been his half-sister, Neferure; on her death after year 23, Sitiah, daughter of the nurse Ipu, became Great Wife. She, in turn, was replaced by Meryetre, the daughter of the Adoratrix Huy. By these ladies, he had up to five sons, and at least two daughters. The eldest son, Amenemhat, died prematurely, but not before receiving a senior government position. Tuthmosis III's heir was accordingly Amunhotpe, born to Meryetre around year 33/4. He was made coregent as Amenophis II, shortly after Tuthmosis' celebration of five decades on the throne, by which time he had also partaken of a number of jubilees.

Although his last expedition into Syria had been eight years previous, Tuthmosis III had not altogether finished with military matters. In year 50, he proceeded into Nubia, clearing the old First Cataract canal of Sesostris III to ease the expedition's passage. He was now, however, well into his sixties, and one month and four days short of the fifty-fourth anniversary of his coronation, Tuthmosis III, in the words of his old comrade-in-arms, Amenemheb, 'completed his lifetime of many years, splendid in valour, might and triumph ... He ascended to the sky, joining the sun, his divine limbs mingling with him that begat him'. Thus passed perhaps Egypt's greatest king, a soldier and a scholar whose name would remain a potent charm for over a thousand years.

His son buried him in his tomb in the Valley of the Kings, the walls of the burial chamber adorned as if a huge papyrus had been unrolled against them. Within, Tuthmosis III was laid to rest in a magnificent quartzite sarcophagus, perhaps the finest of its kind ever made: it was so admired that a thousand years later an Egyptian nobleman named Hapymen would have its decoration copied onto his own coffer, now in the British Museum.

Like so many royal mummies, that of Tuthmosis III was disturbed by robbers, and badly damaged. However, it was salvaged by necropolis officials and moved to the hiding-place at Deir el-Bahari, whence it finally came to rest in the Egyptian Museum, Cairo.

X   The Kings of the Sun

Amenophis III

c. 1388-1348 BC

Tuthmosis III's son, Amenophis II, imitated him in his martial skill, although not his mercy. He was also a considerable builder and sportsman, his prowess being much trumpeted in his inscriptions. He was in turn followed on the throne by Tuthmosis IV, a younger son who may have attained power through the displacement of his elder brother, the *Sem*-Priest of Ptah and probable Crown Prince, Amunhotpe.

Tuthmosis IV's eldest son and successor was Amenophis III, born of Queen Mutemwia. As Crown Prince, he was pictured in the tomb of his tutor, Heqaerneheh, along with a number of his siblings, one of whom, Amenemhat, died young and was buried in Tuthmosis IV's tomb in the Valley of the Kings. King Tuthmosis was also short-lived, and accordingly Amenophis III was barely into his 'teens when he ascended the throne of his ancestors. Within a year or two, however, he had married Tiye, daughter of a chariotry-officer, Yuya, and his wife, Tjuiu, the marriage being marked by the issue of the first of the commemorative scarabs that are a feature of the reign. In his union with a commoner, Amenophis followed Tuthmosis III, Amenophis II, and his own father, in contrast with the kings of the dynasty's earlier years, for whom marriage to a sister seemed *derigueur*.

Building works began early on, as recorded by quarry-inscriptions of the first two years of the reign, while in year 2 scarabs were issued recording a hunt in which the youthful pharaoh is said to have killed ninety-six wild bulls. Year 5 saw the king leading an army through Nubia to put down a rebellion in the far south, possibly the only military operation recorded from the

*Fig. 27. Quartzite head of King Amenophis III, from
his mortuary temple at Thebes; this fragment once
formed part of a standing figure, over 8 metres tall.*

reign. This modest military record contrasts strongly with the
martial spirit of the earlier kings of the dynasty; indeed, study of
the reign of Amenophis III clearly points to there now being far
more attention paid to the arts of peace.

Any desire for physical action on the part of the king seems to
have been assuaged on the hunting field. Following on from the
'Bull-Hunt' scarabs are the 'Lion-Hunt' series, issued to mark the
king's slaughter of over a hundred lions in the first decade of the

reign. A further set of scarabs recorded the arrival of the Mitannian Princess Gilukhepa as diplomatic bride; yet another commemorates the digging of a lake for Queen Tiye in a place still to be identified with certainty.

Amenophis III was a great builder and patron of the arts. A number of temples were founded or re-founded; in particular, the temple of Luxor was erected on a site first occupied under Tuthmosis III. Dedicated to the cult of royal spirit, it is both architecturally and artistically exquisite, its inner rooms containing depictions of the king's divine birth, which make for interesting comparisons with the corresponding scenes of Hatshepsut at Deir el-Bahari. A similar sanctuary was built at Soleb in the Sudan, while Karnak and many other temples were extended and beautified. Indeed, it has recently been recognized that many statues apparently made by Ramesses II are in fact re-carvings of Amenophis III originals.

One would assume that the earlier part of the reign was spent in the north, at the administrative capital of Memphis. However, the second decade seems to have seen the king spending increasing amounts of time at his huge palace on the western side of the river at Thebes, Malqata, where he appears to have been permanently resident from year 29 onwards.

Many of the officials of the reign are known. The Amun-cult at Karnak was headed first by Ptahmose, and then Meryptah, but the position of Second Prophet was held by the king's brother-in-law, Anen. Interestingly enough, we only know of his relationship to the king through his being named as a son on the coffin of Tjuiu, mother of the queen. For much of the reign, the Upper and Lower Egyptian vizierates were respectively held by Ramose and Amunhotpe, the former nevertheless a native of the northern town of Athribis, and close relation of a number of other high officials.

Of these, the most prominent was Amunhotpe-son-of-Hapu, the King's Scribe, and apparent closest advisor. He seems to have been responsible for many of Amenophis III's building projects, including his mortuary temple, and rose to a status without equal amongst the nobility. He was granted a mortuary temple near that of the king, together with a stone sarcophagus of unusual form. Many years after his death, at an age of over 80, he was granted divine honours, and was in Ptolemaic times worshipped alongside

Fig. 28. Three commemorative scarabs of the reign of Amenophis III: from the left, a 'Lake', a 'Marriage' and a 'Lion Hunt' example.

that other deified official and architect, Imhotep, likewise acquiring a reputation for medicine.

It may have been in the 20's of the reign that the king felt the need to turn his attention to the succession. The king and queen are known to have had at least five daughters, and two sons. The elder son was Thutmose, presumably born fairly early in the reign. Rather like his namesake, Tuthmosis III, and a number of other princes since, he was appointed young to priestly office; in this he flourished, rising to the offices of High Priest of Ptah at Memphis, and Overseer of the Priests of Upper and Lower Egypt, the latter effectively putting him in overall charge of Egyptian organized religion. At Memphis, he was responsible for the first known burial of the Apis bull, an incarnation of his god, thus beginning a tradition that was to last until Greek times. All indications are that 'Tuthmosis V' would have been potentially a great king; but it was not to be. The prince-priest died, his place in the succession being taken by his brother, Amunhotpe.

Whether the latter assumed the throne on his father's death, or served for a time as his coregent, has long been debated, with

92

Fig. 29. Glazed steatite statuette of Queen Tiye.

one school advocating such a joint rule beginning around Amenophis III's year 30. A tourist graffito discovered in 1992 at Dahshur might be read as recording Amenophis IV as ruling in a year 32. Unfortunately, the text is very badly damaged, and signs at first thought to be from Amenophis IV's prenomen (Neferkheperure) could be less-controversially interpreted as being from an epithet sometimes found in the nomen of Tuthmosis III. Nevertheless, there remain a number of pieces of evidence which, although equivocal, may point to a fairly long period of joint rule between Amenophis III and IV, including various considerations concerning certain high state-officials of the latter part of Amenophis III's reign. Accordingly, a coregency has been provisionally assumed in compiling the chronology used in this book.

Year 30 apparently saw Amenophis III establishing himself in permanent residence at Thebes, simultaneously celebrating his first jubilee. Huge quantities of potsherds from Malqata record items supplied for the celebration, repeated in years 34 and 37, while elements of its ceremonies appear on temple and tomb walls. Some of the manifestations of the jubilee seem to have been without precedent, including filling the king's mortuary temple, still under construction, with numerous odd animal-sculptures that have recently been suggested as forming part of a massive astronomical tableau.

It would appear that the king's health may have been failing. His mummy shows that he was corpulent and suffered severely

Fig. 30. The Colossi of Memnon, the quartzite statues of Amenophis III that stood at the entrance of his now-vanished mortuary temple.

from dental disease, while a statue of the goddess Ishtar, recorded as having been received by him from his ally, King Tushratta of Mitanni, was perhaps sent for its healing qualities.

In contrast to his physical decline, some of the late depictions of Amenophis III show him as grotesquely young, apparently as an apotheosis of the sun-god Re: the jubilee celebrations seem to have included his elevation to full godhead, with depictions known of the king worshipping himself. It is now being argued strongly that this transformation was directly linked with the new sun-religion championed by his son, Amenophis IV, that of the Aten. Indeed, it may be that Amenophis III *was* the Aten, and that the jubilee of the god celebrated by the younger Amenophis (see below) was in essence identical with one of those of the older king, both marking the latter's rule on earth, but also his transformation into a solar deity.

Little is known of the events of Amenophis III's last few years, apart from the possible implications of his jubilees and the activities of his son. One known action, however, was the elevation of his eldest daughter, Sitamun, to the dignity of King's Great Wife, the same title held by her still-living mother, Tiye. It is unclear whether this 'marriage' involved the king in a physical relationship with his daughter, or whether it simply meant that she took over some of the politico-religious functions of the office; certainly no children may be with any confidence attributed to her.

King Amenophis III died in or around his thirty-ninth regnal year. A tomb had been begun for him in the Western Valley of the Kings back in Tuthmosis IV's reign, and here his mummy was laid to rest, in a huge granite sarcophagus, doubtless surrounded by the riches of what was clearly the most dazzling of Egyptian courts. Almost nothing of these riches survive; the mummy, horrifically damaged by robbers, eventually found its way to the tomb of Amenophis II, and finally the Cairo Museum.

A few kilometres away from the tomb stand a pair of colossal statues, the so-called Colossi of Memnon, which once marked the entrance of the king's mortuary temple, the biggest of its kind ever constructed. An inscription describes it as:

> An august temple on the West of Thebes, an everlasting temple of sandstone, wrought with gold throughout. Its floor

is adorned with silver, its doorways with electrum, very wide and large, established for ever .... It is rich in statues of granite, quartzite and every costly stone .... It is supplied with a 'Station of the King' wrought with gold and many costly stones. Flagstaves are set up before it, covered with electrum, like the horizon in heaven when Re rises within it ....

Alas, all gone. Only the guardian Colossi of Memnon remain, staring faceless into eternity.

Akhenaten and Smenkhkare

c. 1360-1343 BC

Whether the eldest surviving son of Amenophis III came to throne on his father's death, or whether he had previously served as his co-regent has long been a matter of scholarly debate. The options seem to be a short or non-existent overlap, or else a long period of the two monarchs ruling in harness – perhaps for up to a dozen years. On this basis, it would be to the co-regency that one of Amenophis IV's earliest appearances, in the tomb of the vizier, Ramose, at Thebes would date; another early depiction is on a block from the great temple of Amun at Karnak, where he is shown with a falcon-headed god, who is labelled as being a form of Re-Harakhty: 'the Aten'. In these representations, the king is shown in the classical style of his father's reign.

'The Aten' had long been a designation of the physical body of the sun, but during the Eighteenth Dynasty had begun to attain a separate divine status, until under Tuthmosis IV, and still more so under Amenophis III, it had become a considerable deity in its own right. However, under Amenophis IV, the Aten was to be something far more: at first paramount, and then sole god. As a mark of his devotion, early in his reign, the king undertook quarrying at Gebel Silsila to obtain stone for the first great temple of the sun-god Aten, to be erected at Karnak, behind the precinct of Amun-Re. In this building, Amenophis IV is shown with his new consort, one Nefertiti, probably the daughter of the senior army officer, Ay, who may, in turn, have been a brother of Queen Tiye.

Fig. 31. King Akhenaten, with his wife, Nefertiti, and daughters, Meryetaten, Meketaten and Ankhesenpaaten, in the extreme style of his earlier years; from Amarna.

What is remarkable about these depictions is that, unlike the earliest carvings of the king, which are in the purest of traditional styles, they are executed in a manner which, at first sight, contradicts everything that Egyptian art stood for.

Rather than as perfect beings, with admirable figures and features, the king, queen and their entourage are all shown with slack jaws, scrawny features, extravagant paunches, together with swelling hips and breasts. The significance of these distortions, stated by the chief sculptor Bak to have been introduced at the express bidding of the king, remain unclear, but are perhaps intended to show the royal couple as divine beings, rather as were the exaggerations of the late, ultra-youthful, representations of Amenophis III (see p. 95, above). Even more extreme are the series of standing statues of the king which were included in the temple's structure. They mark the apogee of the early, extreme form of what is known as the 'Amarna' style of art. On top of all this, the representation of the Aten in anthropomorphic form was replaced by a depiction of the sun's disk, from which spread down solar rays, each ending in a human hand; the latter hold the sign of 'life' to the nostrils of the king and queen.

The building of the temple coincided with Amenophis IV's celebration of a jubilee; since this was only a handful of years into the reign, this is most unusual, given that most kings waited thirty years before so doing. However, the true celebrant seems not to have been the king, rather the Aten itself. As we have already noted, if Amenophis III and IV were indeed ruling together at this point in time, it will almost certainly have coincided with a jubilee of Amenophis III - whose celebration may have completed his transformation into a solar god. There are indications that these jubilees were intended to signify a fundamental change in the status of the royal family. Henceforth Amenophis III, IV and Queen Nefertiti seem to have formed a trinity of incarnate solar deities, respectively the sun-god, the air-god Shu, and the moisture-goddess Tefnut. As yet, they were operating within the broad boundaries of the traditional Egyptian pantheon; however, that boundary was shortly to be crossed.

In year 5, Amenophis IV made a formal visit to a desolate plain in Middle Egypt, hemmed in on three sides by hills, and by the Nile on the fourth. There, he made a sacrifice and launched into a long proclamation, in which he declared the establishment of a new city, dedicated to the Aten, fulminating against those who opposed his plans, and providing for the institution of festivals for his god. The king's intention that the new town should be the royal seat was reinforced by the announcement that the king, queen and their young daughter, Meryetaten should be buried there, together with all the court. Amid these far-reaching plans, there is a further element of great import: the king is no longer 'Amenophis' ('Amun-is-satisfied'), but 'Akhenaten' ('Incarnation-of-the-Aten'), while the queen adds to her name the sobriquet, Neferneferuaten ('Beautyof-beauties-of-the-Aten'). An account of the visit was carved on three rock-stelae, in the cliffs at the northern and southern extremities of the planned settlement, to be named Akhet-Aten ('Horizon of the Aten') – modern Tell el-Amarna.

Over the next few years, the city grew, with the construction of palaces, temples, government offices and residential quarters – our classic example of Egyptian town-planning in practice. In year 6, the king made a further formal progress around the site, adding additional boundary stelae around the cliffs behind the city and also on the opposite bank of the river, marking out a huge slice of the Nile valley, with the city on one side of the river, and a great area of agricultural land on the other to supply its inhabitants with food. At around this time, Akhenaten's Theban temple finally reached completion, only to be superseded in importance by two great sanctuaries at Amarna, with vast open courts, piled with offerings to the sun.

By this time a second daughter, Meketaten, had been born, with a third, Ankhesenpaaten, arriving around year 7. Three further daughters were subsequently to join the couple's offspring, with at least two boys fathered by Akhenaten with either Nefertiti or another wife. Of such other women, only one is well-known, the Lady Kiya, conceivably the Mitannian princess whom Akhenaten is known to have married as a matter of state. She is named on a number of monuments, and was provided with a fine gilded and inlaid coffin, together with calcite canopic jars before year 9. However, she later fell from grace, had her names erased from monuments, and disappeared from view.

The royal family's role was pivotal in the religion of the Aten. Although the visible globe of the sun might seem the obvious object of a popular devotion, this was not the case. Instead, worship of the universal god could only take place via the royal couple: in private shrines the object of devotion was a stela showing Akhenaten, Nefertiti and their daughters adoring the sun. What was true in life was also true in death: in the tomb chapels cut in the cliffs of Amarna for his officials, it is the royal family and their activities that dominate the scenes, contrasting markedly with the representations of 'daily life' that fill the corresponding tombs at Thebes and elsewhere. A key scene in a number of tombs is the royal family's daily drive, escorted by soldiers, from their residence

Fig. 32. King Akhenaten, in the more naturalistic style of the latter part of his reign.

100

in the far north of the city, along the Royal Road to the palace and temples in the central city.

Up until year 9, the Aten's names, written in twin cartouches, expressed his nature in the terms of other, far older, gods: 'Re-Horus-of-the-horizon lives, who rejoices in the horizon in his name of Shu, who is Aten.' However, after that year the god is 'Re lives, ruler of the horizons, who rejoices in the horizon in his name as Re-the-father, who has returned as Aten'. The nature of the deity is summed up in the great Hymn to the Aten, where it is described as the creator and nurturer of all the peoples and things of the world, who celebrate daily on the globe's appearance on the eastern horizon, and hide in fear when night divides the god from them. By any standards, the Hymn is a great work of poetry, which has been attributed, rightly or wrongly, to the king himself. It has also been likened to the 104th Psalm, there being a number of places where wordings are tantalisingly similar. Modern opinion is, however, that this similarity derives from both works springing from a common Near Eastern cultural milieu, rather than any direct connexion.

Links between Egypt and her neighbours in the ancient world are thrown into sharp relief by the unique survival at Akhet-Aten of letters written to Pharaoh from his vassals and his 'brothers', the kings of the other contemporary Great Powers. This correspondence was on baked clay tablets, written in the Akkadian language (the diplomatic *lingua franca* of the era), expressed in cuneiform script. It seems that even while his father yet lived, Akhenaten had responsibility for dealing with foreign relations; thus, the archive includes a large number of letters addressed to the elder king.

They tell us much of what passed between the potentates of the ancient world, and reveal a picture of endemic squabbling amongst the petty princes of Syria-Palestine, each attempting to further their own interests, at the expense of their fellows. Depending on one's reading of the letters from these princes, one may see a decline in Egyptian power, exacerbated by a gross failure on the part of the pharaoh to act on behalf of his interests in the area. Another view, however, sees merely the usual ebb-and-flow of the influence of Great Powers in an area constantly under dispute.

In the past, it was often thought that Akhenaten had

embraced pacifism as part of his religious creed, and that this lay behind the aforementioned presumed failure to act militarily in the face of attempts to undermine the Egyptian position. That this interpretation is clearly wrong is shown by such scenes as that shown in fig. 33 (cf. p. 104), where his *wife* is shown in a time-honoured royal martial pose. In addition, a later text (p. 109) seems to refer back to military actions under Akhenaten – albeit unsuccessful ones!

Fig. 33. Queen Nefertiti smites an enemy, on a depiction of her barge.

Fig. 34. The ruins of the North Palace at Tell el-Amarna, finally the residence of Meryetaten.

The letters from Akhenaten's 'brothers', the kings of Mitanni, Babylon, the Hittites, Cyprus and Assyria, are more concerned with diplomatic niceties – the negotiation of marriages, and the exchange of gifts. The latter centre on the foreign rulers' desire for gold, since 'gold is as dust in the land of my brother (the pharaoh)'. Interestingly enough, Akhenaten's daughter, Meryetaten, features in a number of letters, symbolic of, as we shall see, her important role towards the end of the reign.

The twelfth year of Akhenaten's reign saw a great durbar at Amarna, when the products of Nubia and the Levant were brought before the enthroned king and queen. The import of this event, precisely dated on the tomb walls that record it, has been much debated, and it is possible that it reflects a celebration that followed Akhenaten's becoming sole king, following Amenophis III's death. This, of course, depends on whether the co-regency could have lasted this long.

We have already seen how the change of Aten's names in year 9 excluded any divine elements other than Re and Aten himself, both direct aspects of the sun. At some point in the reign,

103

quite possibly as soon as the king found himself the throne's sole occupant, a policy of the obliteration of the old religion was adopted. Under this, workmen visited sites throughout Egypt to remove the names and figures of, in particular, Amun-Re, King of the Gods, although other deities suffered, and occasionally the plural word 'gods' itself. This work was sometimes incredibly thorough, with obelisks scaled to remove sculptures from their apexes.

Through all of this time, Queen Nefertiti had been prominent at Akhenaten's side, her status almost the equal of her husband's, at least once shown in the conventional pose of Pharaoh, smiting the enemy (p.102, above). Then, a year or two after the great durbar, she disappears from view. It was once thought she had fallen into disgrace, but this was a case of mistaken identity: it

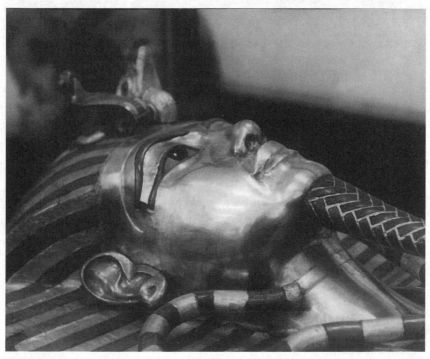

Fig. 35. King Smenkhkare/Neferneferuaten: the portrait-mask of his gilded coffin, later used as part of the funerary equipment of Tutankhamun.

104

was Kiya whose name and images were removed from monuments, and replaced by those of Meryetaten. It is far more likely that Nefertiti had died, at perhaps no more than thirty years of age.

It may not be coincidental that shortly after Nefertiti's disappearance from the archaeological record, Akhenaten acquired a co-regent with whom to share the throne of Egypt. There has been a great deal of discussion as to the identity of this co-ruler, with a whole range of mutually-exclusive theories; one suggestion put forward is that this individual is Nefertiti herself in a new guise – becoming a female king after the models of Sobkneferu and Hatshepsut; another posits two successive co-regents, one a male named Smenkhkare, the other Nefertiti under the name Nefer-neferuaten, both of whom nevertheless shared the same prenomen, Ankhkheperure.

The author's preferred view, however, makes the new joint-pharaoh one person, Akhenaten's elder son (whether by Nefertiti, or a lesser wife), taking the throne under his birth-name, Smenkhkare, at around the age of sixteen. For his coronation, a gigantic brick hall was added to the Great Palace at Amarna, its main room possessing no fewer than five hundred and forty-four square columns, its ceiling painted with grapes and leaves on a yellow ground.

Smenkhkare married his eldest sister, Meryetaten, the young couple being depicted in the tomb of Meryre ii at Amarna, and formerly on a relief from Memphis, where their cartouches appeared along with those of the Aten; the new king was also shown there following his father, on a now-lost relief (fig. 35). The most fascinating thing about Smenkhkare, however, is that – although the son of, and co-ruler with, the founder and guiding light of the Aten-religion – he himself seems to have been a devotee of the old, polytheistic, faith. Although apparently the author of an unfinished tomb at Amarna, the funerary equipment that he began to have made at around the same time bears almost no sign of the sun-cult. The material included a magnificent gilded and inlaid coffin, along with four matching miniature coffinettes to hold his internal organs, all of which invoke Osiris, Isis, and the other traditional deities of burial.

By the time that work had begun in inscribing these

coffinettes, the king had undergone a first change of name, adding elements of Akhenaten's names to his existing cartouches. This amendment was short-lived, for while manufacture continued, his nomen was altered completely, becoming 'Neferneferuaten', which had formed part of the name of the recently-deceased Nefertiti. In spite of these changes of name, perhaps intended to be gestures of loyalty to his father, Neferneferuaten's religious views seem to have continued as before, since in his third year (Akhenaten's sixteenth/seventeenth), we read of the existence of a 'priest and scribe of divine offerings of Amun in the House of Ankhkheperure at Thebes' – presumably his intended mortuary temple, with the implication that he was now planning not to be buried at Amarna, but in the Valley of the Kings.

This whole circumstance sheds considerable light on the true penetration of Atenist art and thought within and without Akhenaten's immediate circle. While it has long been known that many of the ordinary population, even at Amarna, continued to cling to the gods of their ancestors, it may now be seen that not only was the 'counter-reformation' already underway before the Heretic was in the grave, but it was supported by the heir to the throne, who had access to workshops that produced royal funerary equipment of traditional form.

Whatever stresses that sprung from this co-existence of Amun and Aten and their respective royal patrons were suddenly resolved by the death of Neferneferuaten. Whether it was natural or otherwise remains open to speculation. What is clear is that the young king was deprived of the Osirian burial he had sought; instead, Akhenaten had him embalmed in Atenist fashion, without amulets, and buried in a coffin of gilded wood, inscribed with impeccably Atenist texts. The latter was the old coffin of Kiya, in store since her fall from grace, its inscriptions modified to fit a king. With the addition of an Atenist shrine made for Queen Tiye, Kiya's canopic jars, and a sister's lids, Neferneferuaten was probably buried in a tomb at Amarna intended for one or more of his sisters. There he was to rest for perhaps ten years.

The widowed Meryetaten may have served as nominal co-regent for a short while, under the name of Ankh*et*kheperure, a simple feminization of her late husband's prenomen, but the new regime was to be short-lived. Akhenaten himself survived his son by only a few months, dying during his seventeenth regnal year. His body was certainly buried in his great tomb at Amarna, his mummy sheltered by a granite sarcophagus bearing, at its corners, protective figures of his late wife, Nefertiti, shown in a pose more appropriate to the traditional goddesses of burial. Her protection was to be short-lived, however; a decade on, the death of Akhenaten's last son, Tutankhamun, brought to power figures implacably opposed to Akhenaten and his legacy. Soon after Tutankhamun's demise, the royal tombs at Amarna were stripped of their contents; Smenkhkare's body was moved to Thebes, to be buried, deprived of its identity, in a tomb opposite that of his younger brother, where it was to be found in AD 1907. The corpse of Akhenaten has never been positively identified: the burnt remains of a mummy, found outside the door of his tomb, may be all that remained of the Heretic King after his enemies had taken their revenge.

Tutankhamun

c. 1343-1333 BC

Tutankhaten, as he was known when he came to the throne, was almost certainly the younger son of Akhenaten, and once appeared as a prince on a relief, found at Ashmunein and probably originally from Amarna. With the successive deaths of his elder brother and father, the nine or ten year-old boy became king, with his sister Ankhesenpaaten as his queen, and the generals Ay and Horemheb as the effective rulers of the country.

He seems to have spent the first few years of the reign at Amarna, and probably began a tomb there. However, fairly early on, the royal couple's names were changed to Tutankhamun and Ankhesenamun, and the royal residence shifted back to Memphis, for millennia its traditional location. In his earliest years there, the young king was in the charge of a woman named Maya, whose tomb was recently found at Saqqara. Amarna may have remained for a time as the Aten's ceremonial centre and the royal necropolis, but rapid moves were underway to restore the religious status quo.

Fig. 36. One of the numerous statues of Amun produced during Tutankhamun's reign, bearing the features of the king.

108

The key document in this process is the Restoration Stela, now in Cairo. Extracts will suffice to indicate its import:

> Now when His Person had arisen as king, the temples of the gods and goddesses, from Elephantine to the marshes of the Delta ... had fallen into neglect. Their shrines had fallen into desolation and become overgrown with weeds; their sanctuaries were as if they had never been and their halls were a trodden path. The land was in confusion, the gods having forsaken it. If an army was sent to Syria to widen the frontiers of Egypt, it met with no success. If one prayed to a god to ask things of him, he did not come ....
>
> After some time had passed thus, His Person appeared on the throne of his father .... See, His Person was in his palace in the estate of Tuthmosis I ... and took council of his heart, searching out every effective occasion, seeking what was beneficial to his father Amun, for fashioning his august image of real electrum. He has added to what was done in former times, he has fashioned an image of his father Amun upon thirteen carrying-poles, his holy image being of electrum, lapis-lazuli, turquoise and every rare costly stone ....

The text continues, listing the king's numerous benefactions to the gods, thus establishing Tutankhamun as the restorer of the sanctuaries abandoned during Akhenaten's reign. Certainly there are many temple-statues attributable to Tutankhamun's reign, his tenure on the throne being distinguished by a particularly delicate artistic style that combines all the best features of Amarna and traditional work.

Amongst his Theban works were the continuance of the entrance colonnade of Amenophis III's temple at Luxor, complete with associated statues. Karnak was embellished with three-dimensional images of Amun, Amunet and Khonsu, not to mention a whole range of statues and sphinxes depicting the king himself, and a small temple in the king's name. Various fragments at Memphis attest to his buildings there, while at Faras, in Nubia, he was worshipped as a god during his lifetime. Also in the far south, he built a temple at Kawa, from which ultimately came the magnificent pair of granite lions that today flank the entrance to the Egyptian Sculpture Gallery at the British Museum. Finally, his reign apparently saw the first interment of an Apis bull, the bovine

Fig. 37. King Tutankhamun, flanked by the deities Amun-Re and Mut; limestone, from Karnak.

incarnation of the god Ptah, at Saqqara, accompanied by some particularly fine canopic jars and three glass pendants, naming the king.

Nubia was ruled by the Viceroy Huy, well-known from his fine tomb at Thebes. Other high officials were the viziers Usermontju and Pentu, but the most influential were clearly the already mentioned military men, Ay and Horemheb. The former was the probable brother of Tiye and father of Nefertiti, the latter a man of provincial stock who was commander of the army and king's deputy. The treasurer Maya was also a prominent figure, as was Ay's likely son, the General Nakhtmin. Both Maya and Nakhtmin were to present gifts at the king's funeral, while both the former and Horemheb built magnificent tombs at Saqqara. The superb reliefs in Horemheb's tomb include indications of the military expeditions that Horemheb undertook to prove that the blight on campaigning referred to in the Restoration Stela had been removed by Tutankhamun's generous gifts to the gods.

These campaigns were aimed at reasserting Egypt's position amongst her vassals and dependants; they included operations against Libyans, Nubians and Asiatics, the depictions of the prisoners in the tomb of Horemheb providing amazingly accurately studied images of human beings under duress. The reliefs include the victorious Horemheb's reward before Tutankhamun and Ankhesenamun: only a few years later, the general would be king, and shown in the tombs of his followers rewarding them in exactly the same way.

Like all Egyptian kings, Tutankhamun will, in spite of his tender years, have given thought to his tomb. It is known that the Amarna necropolis workmen remained in place for some time into his reign, and it seems very likely that for a number of years it was intended that he be buried there. His planned resting place was most probably a tomb now numbered 29 in the Amarna series, which had reached some forty-five metres into the bedrock before being abandoned. The sarcophagus that had been intended to hold the king's remains had originally been intended to follow Akhenaten's in design, with the queen's figure on ther corners instead of the traditional protective goddesses of burial. After the king's abandonment of Atenism, the great quartzite box was extensively reworked to give his new name, and to convert the figures on its corners to the time-hallowed Isis, Nephthys, Neith and Selqet.

When the decision was made to move the royal tomb-site to Thebes, work must have begun on a new sepulchre in the Valley of the Kings. Regrettably, it is uncertain as to which tomb this was, since it was never finished. The candidates are those later occupied by Kings Ay (WV 23) and Horemheb (KV 57), with the balance of probability favouring the latter. The tomb was left unfinished because, after little more than nine years on the throne, and probably not yet out of his teens, Tutankhamun died. In spite of much speculation, and a number of examinations, no certain conclusions have been reached as to the cause of death, though it is possible that a blow to the head was involved. His two

111

daughters having both been still-born, the male line of the Eighteenth Dynasty died with him.

A tomb in the Valley of the Kings (KV 62), intended for a very high official (Ay?), was appropriated for the king's burial, and after a modest extension received his mummy and funerary equipment. The latter included a number of items, including a coffin and the canopic coffinettes, that had been long ago made for Neferneferuaten, but discarded by Akhenaten.

After a ritual meal, the debris of which, together with the refuse from the king's embalming, was placed just inside the tomb's entrance, the latter was sealed and, apart from two minor intrusions, was to remain closed until 1922, when Howard Carter's excavations revealed the tomb and its treasures to the world.

Ay

c. 1333-1328 BC

Ay first appears in history as Master of Horse at the court of Akhenaten. His tomb was intended to be one of the largest at Amarna, and reflects his high status. There is no evidence for his having held any priestly office and, like most of the men of power at the end of the dynasty, he was first and foremost a soldier.

Although we have no explicit statement of the fact, it is likely that Ay hailed from Akhmim, where he was to cut a rock-chapel to the local god, Min. It is also likely that he was a relation, if not the son, of another Akhmim worthy: Yuya, the father of Queen Tiye. As a brother-in-law of Amenophis III, his prominence would be easily explicable. In addition, however, there is circumstantial evidence of his being the father of Queen Nefertiti, thus further reinforcing his position at court.

At Tutankhaten's accession, Ay retained his high status and, on that king's death ascended the throne, probably as the man with the closest royal connexions left alive. He is shown as king presiding over the funeral of Tutankhamun on the wall of the latter's burial chamber, presumably to make explicit his accession by virtue of being Horus granting proper burial to his father, Osiris.

Fig. 38. A wall from the tomb of Ay (WV 23). Uniquely, he included a scene of fishing and fowling in his burial chamber, a double break with tradition, as such motifs are otherwise found only in mortuary chapels, and then only those of private persons.

His need to make such an outright statement of his legitimacy is well explained by the events which immediately followed Tutankhamun's death. As we learn from the Hittite archives, the widowed Queen Ankhesenamun wrote to Suppiliumas, the Hittite king, requesting one of his sons, for her to marry and make pharaoh. As one might imagine, this request came as something of a surprise, and it was only after Hittite agents had confirmed the truth of Tutankhamun's lack of a son that a prince, one Zannanza, was despatched.

He never arrived in Egypt, being killed en-route through Syria, leaving Ay to become undisputed king on the day he conducted Tutankhamun's funeral. This event appears to have taken place some eight months after his death, delayed well beyond the traditional seventy days by the diplomatic and political manoeuvrings of the 'Hittite Option'. Although a finger-ring, now in Berlin, associates Ankhesenamun's name with that of Ay, the former

113

rapidly disappears from history. Her dealings with the Hittites may have been regarded as verging on the treasonable, and there are cases where her name and figure have been hacked from a monument, indicating her disgrace.

Ay's accession marked the definitive break with the heritage of Akhenaten, with the dismantling of the Amarna royal cemetery soon after Tutankhamun's demise, and the likely destruction of the Heretic's body. Little is known of the events of the reign, although its major figures continued in office from Tutankhamun's regime.

Ay died after a reign of only four years, being by then at least seventy years old; the king's son, Nakhtmin, seems to have died fairly early in the reign, for we soon find Horemheb holding the titles of the royal heir. Either then, or directly after Ay's death, Horemheb had married Mutnodjmet, sister of Nefertiti, and like her almost certainly Ay's daughter.

The king built his mortuary temple at Medinet Habu, and had WV 23 prepared for his burial in the West Valley of the Biban el-Moluk, a tomb which may have been begun for Neferneferuaten and/or Tutankhamun. His burial there by Horemheb seems to have been somewhat perfunctory, and in later years his memory suffered the same affronts as those of Akhenaten and his sons.

Horemheb

c. 1328-1298 BC

Horemheb first appears unequivocally on the scene under Tutankhamun, as army chief and King's Deputy, although some have recognized an earlier incarnation in a Troop Commander Paatenemheb, who had begun a tomb at Amarna that was never completed. Horemheb's close colleague, Maya, almost certainly served Akhenaten at Amarna, probably being identical with one May, who also owned a tomb at the Heretic's capital. These two men had superbly decorated tombs built for themselves at Saqqara during the reigns of Tutankhamun and Ay, cleared since 1975 by the United Kingdom's Egypt Exploration Society and the

National Museum of Antiquities, Leiden, in the Netherlands. During the late Eighteenth Dynasty, Saqqara had begun to rival Thebes as the burial place of major figures in the national administration, at least one vizier of Amenophis III having previously been buried there.

Horemheb can be seen as Ay's heir on a relief from the tomb of the High Priest of Ptah, Ptahemhat-Ty, and shortly afterwards as king, on his coronation statue, now in Turin. The inscription on this piece, which shows Horemheb together with Mutnodjmet, gives a summary of his earlier career, and then recounts how his local god, Horus of Hnes, elevated him to the throne. Whether this is intended to record his nomination as heir by Ay (as king, an incarnation of Horus), is simply a figure of speech, or should be seen as a

Fig. 39. Horemheb, depicted while still only a General, in his tomb at Saqqara. After his accession, a uraeus was added to his brow to signify his assumption of kingship.

justification of his having won some struggle for power on Ay's death is wholly unclear.

Although some Akhenaten material had begun to be dismantled back in the time of Tutankhamun, and major attacks on Akhenaten's memory begun immediately after Tutankhamun's death, it was with Horemheb that the first attempts seem to have been made to write the Amarna Period out of history. A statue-base of Horemheb is known from the city of Amarna itself, indicating some continuing official occupation there, but this was probably accompanied by the demolition of many buildings for stone to reuse. Most definitely, the Aten-temples at Karnak were taken down and immediately employed in the foundations and filling of Horemheb's own erections to Amun-Re. In particular these building programmes included the commencement of the mammoth Hypostyle Hall, and the addition of the Ninth and Tenth Pylons. At Luxor, he continued the work of Amenophis III and Tutankhamun, usurping the latter's monuments both here and elsewhere: many of the statues and reliefs today bearing Horemheb's cartouches were actually made for Tutankhamun.

As might be expected by a former general, some military operations were undertaken during Horemheb's reign, perhaps following on from those which he had carried out under his predecessors, but they seem to have been of strictly limited extent. Reliefs on the north face of the Tenth Pylon and on the adjacent courtyard wall attest to a Syrian campaign, but little is known of it, nor a Nubian operation also depicted in the king's rock-cut sanctuary at Silsila. The Karnak inscriptions also provide evidence of trade-contact with Punt.

The domestic leitmotif of the reign is apparently given by the Edict which was presumably promulgated early on, although no date survives. Inscribed on a stela on the north face of the Tenth Pylon at Karnak, with a duplicate known from Abydos, it describes the king's desire to remedy various excesses committed by servants of the state. Its provisions detail the harsh punishments to be borne by those who transgressed the royal will: official extorters faced the removal of their noses and then exile; soldiers who stole animal-hides would receive a hundred blows and five open wounds. Further measures guard against official bribery and corruption, the whole document giving the impression of a coordinated body of laws intended to stamp out widespread arbitrary excess on the part of state officialdom. The background to this decree is generally seen as the result of the iconoclastic policy of Akhenaten, whose disruption of the traditional temple-based economy had opened the door to all kinds of excesses by *arriviste* local administrators and soldiery. However, by the time Horemheb came to the throne, Akhenaten had been dead for some fifteen years and, moreover, for the vast majority of this period, Horemheb had been at the head of events.

In view of this fact, one may validly question whether the Edict actually refers to the period directly preceding Horemheb's ascent of the throne. One option is to see it as the king's recounting of reforms he had overseen as an official of Tutankhamun, without stating the fact. The alternative is that the entire stela was the work of Tutankhamun: nowhere in the body of the text is the king's name mentioned, its attribution being due to the appearance of Horemheb's name on the lunette (rounded upper part of the stela). Now, as we have seen, Horemheb is the frequent usurper of Tutankhamun's monuments; might this not be the case here? Regrettably, the lunette is now lost, so we are unable to check the originality of the cartouche. Some scholars have claimed that the language used in the stela supports Horemheb's authorship; however, the short time-difference involved makes this rather less than certain.

That some lawlessness existed during Horemheb's reign is shown by the robbery and restoration of the tomb of Tuthmosis IV in Horemheb's eighth regnal year. The graffiti recording the restoration shows it to have been in the hands of the Treasurer Maya, who had a few years earlier contributed to the burial of Tutankhamun. He was also probably responsible for the re-closure of the latter's tomb, which also seems to have suffered from the attention of robbers during Horemheb's time. Maya died not many years later, and was interred in his magnificently decorated tomb at Saqqara, which lay alongside that of his erstwhile colleague, and now monarch, Horemheb. Also at Saqqara, two of the series of Apis burials, inaugurated by Prince Thutmose B back in the reign of Amenophis III, are attributable to Horemheb's reign, buried in two rooms of a single tomb. One room of this sepulchre was found intact in 1852.

As a private individual, Horemheb had begun to construct a tomb of the largest dimensions at Saqqara, work continuing through the reigns of both Tutankhamun and Ay. Reliefs of the very highest quality were recovered from its ruins in the nineteenth century, the tomb itself being finally located and excavated in 1975. On Horemheb's accession, uraei were added to the brows of his figures there, and perhaps there was a brief thought of making it his regal tomb as well. However, a tomb of conventional royal type was eventually begun in the Kings' Valley, and the former mortuary temple of Ay taken over and rebuilt on a much larger scale. The old tomb seems to have been used for the burial of his first wife, Amenia, who died during Ay's reign, as well as his second, and queen, Mutnodjmet. Bones found in one part of the substructure seem to show that, in poor health and aged around forty-five, Nefertiti's sister had lost her life in attempting to give birth to a final child, probably in the thirteenth year of Horemheb's reign. Of earlier offspring, none seem to have survived their father.

The decoration of Horemheb's Theban tomb was still unfinished at his death. The exact length of his reign is unclear, the highest unequivocal date being in the thirteenth year. However, a twenty-seventh year mentioned in a graffito on a statue in his mortuary temple is in all probability Horemheb's and may come close to the end of his life. Some bones that survived when his tomb in the Valley of the Kings was first opened may have been those of the king, but they do not seem to have been examined, and their location is now unknown.

Dying without surviving issue, Horemheb was the last king of the Eighteenth Dynasty. As his successor he chose Paramesse, his (probably Northern) Vizier, who accordingly became Ramesses I, the founder of a new, Nineteenth, Dynasty.

XI   The Power and the Glory

Sethos I

c. 1296-1279 BC

The dynastic founder, General Paramesse, had been a colleague of
Horemheb while the latter was still serving as army commander,
and is perhaps shown in Horemheb's Saqqara tomb being
rewarded by the King's Deputy. Paramesse was the son of a Troop
Commander, Sethy, and thus was continuing a family military
tradition. A military officer Ramose, who had a tomb at Amarna
may, or may not, be him in his earlier years (Paramesse is simply
'Ramose' with the definitive article added at the beginning). During
the post-Akhenaten reigns, Paramesse rose in army rank before
ultimately receiving the civil office of (presumably Northern) Vizier.
His high status was confirmed by the further office of Overseer of
Priests of Upper and Lower Egypt, thus placing him at the head of
the civil and sacerdotal administrations.

Finally, he became King's Deputy and Executive, the titles
that had lain behind Horemheb's own accession to the throne; he
may have served briefly as Horemheb's co-regent, on the basis of
an obelisk-fragment in Edinburgh, but in any case succeeded him
on the throne as King Ramesses I. As such, he took a prenomen
reminiscent of that of Amosis (*Men*pehtire vs. *Neb*pehtire), thus
asserting a claim to initiating a new era: Akhenaten was now a
creature of the past.

Ramesses married one Sitre, whose antecedents are unknown; their only known child was Sethy, who on his father's accession became the heir to the throne. Shown by an inscription
on a statue-base from Medamud to have been his father's co-
regent, he led an expedition to Palestine during the last months of
Ramesses I's reign; an old man, the elder king's death occurred

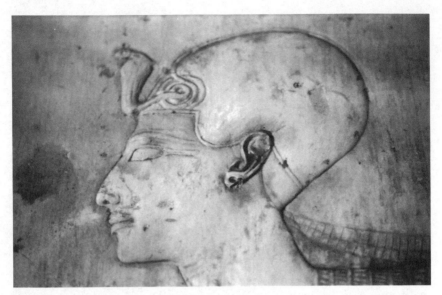

Fig. 40. King Sethos I, as shown in his temple at Abydos. The reign of Sethos was a high-point in New Kingdom art.

less than two years after his appearance on the throne of Two Lands. His tomb had only been begun recently, and it was necessary to improvise a burial chamber far smaller than had been intended, with a sarcophagus decorated only in yellow paint.

The first year of the reign of Sethos I saw a major campaign into Palestine, recorded on the outside walls of the Hypostyle Hall at Karnak, begun by Horemheb and continued by the Ramessides. Information is also contained in a stela from Beth-shan, for some time a major Egyptian centre in Palestine. The initial thrust was up the coast to Gaza, securing the wells along the main trade route, and then taking that town, before pressing on further north. The territory up to the area of Tyre seems then to have been pacified, before the king returned to the fortress of Tjel, in the north-east Delta.

Further campaigns in the immediately succeeding seasons pushed up deeper into Palestine and southern Syria, coming into conflict with the Hittites in securing the city of Qadesh, Tuthmosis III's old opponent. Dominion over that town soon lapsed, however, with a balance of influence and power in the area

120

established between the Hittite and Egyptian kingdoms by the sixth year of the reign. Some warfare had also proven necessary on the western frontier against the Libyans; in this campaign, we first come across the young Crown Prince, Ramesse. His figure was secondarily inserted into the Karnak reliefs, replacing that of Mehy, who seems to have been Sethos I's senior field-commander during his foreign wars.

After the settling of affairs in the north, military intervention became necessary in Nubia in year 8, when a rebellion was hatched in Irem. A force was despatched into the far south, and a seven-day campaign was sufficient to crush the insurrection and carry off over six hundred prisoners.

Fig. 41. King Sethos I in his chariot, preceded by his prisoners from his Levantine campaign. The small figure behind the vehicle is that of his son, Ramesse (later Ramesses II), carved over an earlier image of the General Mehy (exterior of Hypostyle Hall, Karnak).

121

As a discerning patron of the arts, Sethos was one of the most outstanding kings of Egyptian history. Fine relief-sculpture adorned the new Karnak Hypostyle Hall, but the pinnacle was reached at his seven-sanctuaried temple at Abydos. The painted reliefs on the walls of this building rank as perhaps the finest work carried out at any time in Egypt. Their amazingly delicate carving, exquisite detail and fine colouring quite clearly point to an intense personal royal interest in the decoration of the temple. The Abydos temple was accompanied by a curious cenotaph, the Osireion, presumably intended to allow the king to have a post-humous presence in the holy city of Osiris, much as had Sesostris III and Amosis in previous centuries.

These high standards can be seen throughout the artistic output of the reign, with both two- and three-dimensional sculpture of the king closely approaching portraiture – as may be seen by comparing the head of the king's mummy with them. The contrast between this work, and that of the reigns of Sethos' successors, can also be seen at Abydos, where the outer parts of the temple, and its accompanying cenotaph, were completed and decorated after his death.

An interesting episode is recalled by an inscription in the chapel of Wadi Abbad, in the desert over fifty kilometres east of Edfu. This records the digging of a well for the benefit of gold miners coming back to the Nile valley from their work in the Eastern Desert. Another text in the same place contains a stern warning to any future ruler who might seek to upset arrangements made by Sethos to ensure the endowments of his Abydos temple:

> As for any future kings who shall overthrow any of my plans ..., [the gods] will redden like fire to burn up the limbs of those who have not listened to me ....
>
> As for any official who shall suggest to his lord that [temple-]personnel should be given to another service through injudicious counsels, the fire shall burn him: the fire will burn up his limbs ....

While yet a commoner, Sethos I had married Tuya, daughter of Raia, a chariotry officer and his wife, Ruia. They had three known children, a son, Ramesse, and two daughters, Tjia and Henutmire. Tjia married a senior official, named Tia, while her sister would many years later take the titles of a royal wife. Ramesse was to succeed his father as king.

The exact length of Sethos' reign is unclear, but all indications are that it was something between fifteen and twenty years in duration. At his death, he was laid to rest in his tomb in the Valley of the Kings, a wonderfully decorated monument that is now suffering terribly from the effects of the modern environment. Sethos' alabaster outer coffin is now in Sir John Soane's Museum, Lincoln's Inn Fields, London, his mummy in the Cairo Museum.

Ramesses II

c. 1279-1212 BC

During the Eighteenth Dynasty, royal princes had rarely featured on public monuments, Tuthmosis III's son, Amenemhat, and Crown Prince Thutmose, under Amenophis III, being amongst the relatively few exceptions. However, under Sethos I, his heir, Ramesse, was depicted in a number of ritual scenes with his father in the Abydos temple, in particular reading out the long list of ancient kings to whom offering is being made.

As was usual practice, his status had been publicly confirmed by Sethos, and this was later followed by his proclamation as co-regent. The length of time occupied by this joint-rule is uncertain, but on his father's death, Ramesses II was to embark on a reign that was to last sixty-seven years, the longest properly-documented period of rule known from Egyptian history.

The first three years of the king's independent reign – which he numbered from the death of his father, in contrast to most earlier and later kings who had served as co-regents – seem to have been mainly concerned with building. Four months into his first year saw the king setting out on a voyage from Thebes, where he had spent the time since Sethos I's burial planning new works and settling new appointments, bound for the eastern Delta, where a new capital, Piramesse ('The House of Ramesses'), was to be founded on part of the site of the old Hyksos stronghold of

Fig. 42. Ramesses II while yet Crown Prince (temple of Sethos I at Abydos).

Avaris. En route, he stopped at Abydos and ordered the completion of his father's temple, work on which appeared to have stopped on Sethos' demise.

Much of the outer part of this temple comprises Ramesses II's work, the decoration well illustrating the difference between the artistic standards of the old and new reigns. Rather than the delicate low-relief of Sethos I, a cruder sunk-relief is used; here, as was to be the case throughout Egypt and Nubia, quality was sacrificed in the name of quantity and speed. Building work also proceeded rapidly at Thebes, where the basic construction of a new forecourt and pylon for the Luxor temple, built by Amenophis III, was complete by year 3, awaiting decoration.

The fourth regnal year marked the beginning of Ramesses' independent campaigning into the Levant. An initial operation regained territory lost during Sethos I's reign, establishing a jumping-off point for the recapture of Qadesh, for so long regarded by Egypt as being the key to the domination of Syria. Unluckily for

124

Fig. 43. The pylon of the temple of Luxor, decorated with scenes of the Battle of Qadesh. The temple was begun by Amenophis III and completed by Ramesses II. The obelisk that formerly stood to the right of the entrance is now in Place de la Concorde, Paris.

Ramesses, the Hittites were equally convinced of the desirability of holding the city, and a large army was put together by King Muwatallis II to oppose the Egyptians.

Year 5 marked Ramesses' departure for Syria, heading the four divisions of the army, named for the gods Amun, Re, Ptah and Seth. Arriving a month later some way south of Qadesh, he was convinced by a pair of local tribesmen that Muwatallis was far away to the north, in the area of Aleppo. Acting on this apparently good intelligence that the enemy main body was nearly 200 kilometres away, Ramesses pressed on with the Amun-division to pitch camp just north-west of Qadesh. There they prepared to launch an attack once the remaining three divisions, following separately at a considerable distance, had joined.

However, shortly afterwards two captured Hittite scouts revealed that not only was the Hittite king nowhere near Aleppo, but that he was with his army about three kilometres away, on the opposite side of Qadesh! Messages were sent to the Re- and Ptah-divisions warning them of the situation and urging haste; the Seth-division was still too far distant to be of help. Meanwhile, non-combatants were sent away, led by Prince Prehirwenemef.

The Hittites chariot-force struck as the Re-division approached the royal camp. Spread out across the plain, the Egyptian line was broken and the division smashed. The enemy then swung around to attack the king and the Amun-division, whose troops rapidly fell into disorder. The day was saved only by a series of counter-charges by Ramesses and his household troops and, perhaps most importantly, the arrival of a force of Egyptian auxiliary troops from the Syrian coast.

Faced with this, the Hittites evidently felt that a tactical withdrawal would be prudent, which rapidly lost its order and turned into an abject flight, men and equipment being lost in crossing the river Orontes, that separated them from King Muwatallis and their infantry divisions. At the same time, the Ptah-division arrived, thus leaving the battlefield in Ramesses' hands, reinforced at sunset by the final Egyptian division, that of Seth.

Renewal of the battle the next morning led to stalemate, as a result of which Muwatallis proposed a truce. This was accepted for the time being, and early in Ramesses' year 6 the Egyptian forces returned home, having signally failed in their purpose – the capture of Qadesh and the surrounding territory. This was further brought home by the subsequent Hittite occupation of territory that had hitherto been Egyptian. On the other hand, the Hittites were discomfited by the Assyrian conquest of their ally Hanigalbat, the rump of the former Mitannian state.

In spite of the less than favourable strategic outcome, the Qadesh campaign was widely publicised by Ramesses II. Versions were inscribed on the walls of the king's numerous new temples, amongst the most spectacular of which was that carved into the living rock at Abu Simbel in Nubia.

Further military action followed in years 7 to 10, starting off with the Syrian coast, but then pushing deep into Hittite-held territory. In this Ramesses was probably helped by the death of King Muwatallis II and the insecurity of his successor Urhiteshub (Mursilis III). On Egypt's western borders, Libyan incursions were deterred by a series of fortresses; in the south, a campaign was necessary above the third cataract, but otherwise all appears to have been peaceful in the near-abroad.

In the north, however, year 16 saw a *coup d'etat* in the Hittite state, which brought Hattusilis III to the throne, and pushed Urhiteshub into exile, the latter finally making his way to Egypt. A Hittite demand for his extradition was refused, and war appeared likely. However, a sudden Assyrian advance presented Hattusilis with a far closer threat than Egypt, leading to peace between himself and Ramesses being seen as a preferred option.

Accordingly, in year 21 a formal peace treaty was agreed between the two powers, inscribed in cuneiform on a tablet of silver. Copies survive both on clay tablets in the Hittite archives in Boghazköi, and in hieroglyphs in the temple of Karnak, and show that, territorially, the *status quo* was recognized, with Qadesh remaining in Hittite hands. On the other hand, Egypt's rights of access to her various Syrian coastal trading-partners and allies were guaranteed, with both powers agreeing a non-aggression pact and mutual security against third parties. Extradition terms were covered, with guarantees as to the treatment of those extradited – doubtless inspired by the matter of Urhiteshub, which had so nearly brought the new allies to the brink of war. The former Mursilis III was evidently not, however, affected by the treaty,

Fig. 44. The Great Temple at Abu Simbel, carved out of the sandstone cliff by Ramesses II.

remaining at the Egyptian court, and being the cause of occasional friction between the two monarchies.

The agreement of the treaty was marked by correspondence between both the kings, and their wives, Pudukhepa and Nefertiry, together with the exchange of presents that formed the underpinning of much ancient diplomacy. A further aspect of such international relationships was brought into play a dozen years later when negotiations began for the marriage of Hattusilis III's eldest daughter with Ramesses II; in year 34, she arrived in Egypt, to become the third King's Great Wife of the reign, under the new Egyptian name of Maahorneferure.

Two ladies had held the title of 'Great Wife' at the beginning of the reign, the aforementioned Nefertiry, and Isetnofret (A). There is no certain evidence that either had royal blood, although a fragment of furniture from Nefertiry's tomb might suggest some relationship with the late King Ay. Nefertiry was initially the more prominent, receiving the honour of a rock-cut temple at Abu Simbel, small only in relation to the gigantic sanctuary of her husband, a few metres to the south. She died soon after year 24, being buried in a magnificent tomb in the Valley of the Queens. Interestingly, she is shown there, most unusually for Egyptian art, with a pink complexion. One of the few other examples is the well-known Berlin head of Queen Nefertiti, the putative daughter of Ay: might this link in with the Ay material found in Nefertiry's tomb?

Isetnofret seems to have outlived her fellow queen by about ten years. Their roles as 'King's Great Wives' were taken by their eldest daughters, Nefertiry's Meryetamun, and Isetnofret's Bintanat (a Canaanite name), joined in year 35 by the Hittite Maahorneferure, and still later by their sister, Nebettawy. Bintanat, at least, fulfilled the biological role of 'wife' to her father as well as the ceremonial functions of the title. It is unclear, however, whether this was always the case with father-daughter marriages, as we have seen (p. 95), the point being moot concerning Sitamun under Amenophis III.

Nefertiry and Isetnofret bore numerous children to their husband, supplemented by the offspring of the many other members of the king's harem: ultimately, around a hundred and fifty progeny were born to him. A series of sons held the title of Crown Prince, beginning with Amenhirwenemef, later re-named Amenhirkopshef (A). On his death, he was followed in turn by his younger brothers, Sethhirkopshef, Ramesse, and Khaemwaset, before Merenptah succeeded in living long enough to follow his father on the throne.

Of these princes, Khaemwaset was to exceed the fame of all his siblings, and challenge his father in the memory of posterity. His fame, for wisdom and magical skill was to subsist for a thousand years after his death, stories woven round him being preserved in demotic papyri from Ptolemaic and Roman times, and are still being recycled in modern literature. His career was to closely mirror that of the earlier Prince Thutmose B (p. 92): he was intimately involved with the burials of the Apis bulls, he was to eventually hold the titles of Crown Prince and High Priest of Ptah; finally, he was also to predecease his father, depriving Egypt again of a potentially outstanding pharaoh.

Khaemwaset also has a claim to having been the earliest known Egyptologist. It is clear from their tourist graffiti that the ancient Egyptians of the New Kingdom took an interest in their past; Khaemwaset is known to have discovered a statuette of Kawab, son of Kheops, and placed it in the temple, suitably inscribed. He also inscribed on the casing stones of pyramids the names and titles of their owners. On the debit side, however, it seems fairly certain that this work was often done while the ancient monuments underwent partial demolition for reusable stone, in which case Khaemwaset's work might be likened to that of modern 'rescue archaeologists', employed to mitigate the effects of the building work associated with 'progress'.

The names and titles of many of the members of the administration are known. The Lower Egyptian vizierate was held successively by Pramessu, Sethy, Prahotpe i and Prahotpe ii; their southern colleagues were Paser (a particularly well-attested figure, son of the late High Priest of Amun, Nebnetjeru and later to be High Priest of Amun himself) and Neferrenpet i. The High Priesthood of Amun was in the hands of Nebwennenef (who was to be given the signal honour of a West Theban mortuary temple), and then Wennefer, the aforementioned Paser, Bakenkhonsu (who had previously successively held the subordinate posts of Fourth, Third and Second Prophet of Amun) and, finally, the latter's brother, Roma-Roy, who remained in office until the fall of the later King Amenmesse.

The other great High Pontificates, of Ptah at Memphis, and Re at Heliopolis, were graced by the appointment of royal princes at certain points during the reign. The 'Greatest of Craftsmen', to quote the Memphite priest's proper title, included Pahemnetjer i and ii, Merenptah, Huy, Prince Khaemwaset, Rahotpe, Ptahem-akhet i and Neferrenpet ii. The final pontiff of the reign may have been Hori, son of Prince Khaemwaset; of course, if his father had not predeceased the king, Hori would have been in line for the throne. At Heliopolis, Bak and Amenemopet were followed by Prince Meryatum A, thus placing the two major northern cults very firmly under royal control during the middle years of the reign.

The Egyptian-Hittite alliance appears to have held firm, a manifestation being a trip to Egypt by the Crown Prince Hishimisharruma, the future King Tudkhalias IV. A state visit by

130

Hattusilis III himself was also planned, but it is unclear whether it actually took place, although there is no doubt that a further Anatolian princess was sent to Egypt as a bride for Ramesses II.

As was customary, the thirtieth year of the reign saw the king's jubilee – the first of fourteen such celebrations that were to occur at regular intervals during Ramesses' lifetime. The first celebration was especially marked by building work, just one element of a long-term constructional programme that exceeded that of any other pharaoh. Almost every site in Egypt preserves some fragment of the reign's constructions, either additions to standing structures or wholly new ones. Amongst the most significant temple-sites, apart from the already-encountered Abu Simbel, Abydos and Luxor, are Heliopolis, Memphis (where a wholly-new Ptah-temple was erected), Herakleopolis, Antinoë, Ashmunein, Akhmim, Meshayikh, Koptos, Karnak, El-Kab, Beit el-Wali, Gerf Husein, Wadi es-Sebua, Derr and Napata, the latter five being in Nubia.

Another great work of the reign was the king's mortuary temple at Western Thebes, known today as the Ramesseum. One of the largest of its kind, its pylon was decorated with an account of the Qadesh campaign, with its courtyards adorned with numerous huge statues. One, the 'Young Memnon' is now a well-known exhibit at the British Museum, while another's remains are immortalised in Shelley's sonnet, 'Ozymandias' (a Classical corruption of Ramesses II's prenomen):

> I met a traveller from an antique land
> Who said: 'Two vast and trunkless legs of stone
> Stand in the desert. Near them, on the sand,
> Half-sunk, a shattered visage lies, whose frown,
> And wrinkled lip, and sneer of cold command,
> Tell that its sculptor well those passions read
> Which yet survive, stamped on these lifeless things,
> The hand that mocked them, and the heart that fed:
> And on the pedestal these words appear:
> 'My name is Ozymandias, king of kings;
> Look on my works, ye Mighty, and despair!'
> Nothing beside remains. Round the decay
> Of that colossal wreck, boundless and bare,
> The lone and level sands stretch far away.'

The king's last years, during which he may have reached his nineties, were plagued by dental problems, arthritis and arteriosclerosis. Death finally came in the sixty-seventh year of his reign, Ramesses II finding rest in the tomb he had long ago prepared for himself in the Valley of the Kings. Today the tomb is a sad wreck, severely damaged by flooding, and preserving almost nothing of what must have been one of the most opulent of all royal burials. As with almost all of the other kings of the New Kingdom, the mummy was later moved, being found in the Deir el-Bahari cache in a coffin that had once been that of his grandfather, Ramesses I.

Ramesses II's funeral was performed by his thirteenth, and eldest surviving, son, Merenptah. Already well into his fifties or sixties, he had been heir since the death of his brother, Khaemwaset, nearly a dozen years previously, and must have shouldered many of the practical aspects of the monarchy during his father's declining years. He was thus well equipped to take the throne in his own right, albeit at an age where he could not expect a reign anywhere approaching the length of Ramesses II's!

XII   The Feud of the Ramessides

Sethos II and Amenmesse

c.1201-1195 BC

The decade occupied by the reign of Ramesses II's successor, Merenptah, was an eventful one. In particular, an invasion of 'Sea Peoples', who were a coalition of Libyans and Mediterranean peoples, had to be repulsed in the fifth year of his reign, while, more peaceably, grain was shipped to the Hittites to relieve a famine, presumably a manifestation of continued alliance between the Egyptian and Anatolian peoples.

Merenptah's heir was Prince Sethy-Merenptah (A), who may be seen depicted, with the titles of Executive, Royal Scribe, Generalissimo and Crown Prince, on a considerable number of his father's statues, as well as in battle-scenes where, given Merenptah's advanced age, he may have been in actual charge. Thus on his father's death he assumed the throne as Sethos II. Probably already in his fifties, he began work on his tomb in the Valley of the Kings, documents dated to his first and second regnal years surviving in the archives at Deir el-Medina. However, at this point, King Sethos suddenly disappears from the Theban record, his place apparently filled by one Amenmesse.

Much debate has surrounded King Amenmesse, both concerning his origins, and his exact position in the late Nineteenth Dynasty. As to the former, there is evidence that he was a son of Sethos II, by his principal wife, Takhat, a younger daughter of Ramesses II, and thus her husband's aunt. He also appears to have served Merenptah as Viceroy of Kush, under the name Messuy: representations of the latter at Amada in Nubia show this worthy with a uraeus added to his brow.

Fig. 45. A quartzite statue of King Amenmesse, later usurped by
Sethos II (Hypostyle Hall, Karnak); the head of the statue is now
Metropolitan Museum of Art, New York.

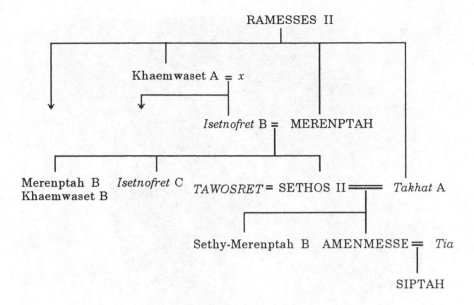

Fig. 46. *Genealogical table for the later Nineteenth Dynasty.*

As regards his position, one view gives him an independent reign directly after Merenptah's death; the other, adopted here, places his usurpation within the reign of his putative father. Since Sethos II's intended heir seems to have been a Prince Sethy-Merenptah B, it would seem likely that Amenmesse's seizure of power was an attempt to displace his elder brother from the succession, particularly in view of their father's relatively advanced age. If so, it seems to have been only partially successful, for Amenmesse's rule does not appear to have extended as far north as Memphis which, together with the delta and the dynastic seat of Piramesse, would seem to have remained in the hands of Sethos II.

Nevertheless, Amenmesse is well attested in and around Thebes, where he began his tomb, adorned the temple of Karnak with a number of fine statues, and where the old High Priest, Roma-Roy appears to have been one of his adherents, and undertook work in a number of sanctuaries. His undisputed control of Nubia, not surprising if he had indeed previously served as Viceroy, is displayed by a chapel erected in his honour at Amara

135

*Fig. 47. Queen Takhat, wife of Sethos II and mother of Amenmesse (as
shown on the side of the statue depicted in figure 45).*

136

West and a rock-cut stela at Abu Simbel.

The period of Amenmesse's rule saw a number of dramatic events within the workmen's community at Deir el-Medina. These concerned the Chief Workman, Neferhotpe, and his foster son, Paneb. The latter was a hot-headed individual, who had made a number of violent threats against Neferhotpe, and other members of the community. Paneb was successfully prosecuted by his father in the court of the vizier Amenmose, and suffered punishment at the latter's hands. Paneb, however, later gained his revenge, succeeding in persuading King Amenmesse to dismiss the vizier, the head of the government; shortly afterwards, Neferhotpe was murdered. Paneb thereafter crowned his remarkable political feat by being elevated to Chief Workman, and continued on a career of fraud, rape and theft until apparently removed from office around the end of the dynasty, some ten years later.

Amenmesse's irregular rule was brought to an end in his fourth regnal year. Nothing is known of the events that surrounded his disappearance from the scene; all that is certain is that Sethos II regained control of the whole country, and set about the removal of Amenmesse's names wherever they occurred. A number of officials associated with the displaced usurper also seem to have lost their jobs, most notably the Theban High Priest, Roma-Roy, who was followed in the office by the former royal secretary, Mahuhy, who himself soon fell from grace and was replaced by one Minmose.

Most of Amenmesse's monuments were appropriated in Sethos' name, many pieces so thoroughly that hardly any sign of the original cartouches remains. More remarkable, however, is the treatment meted out to Amenmesse's tomb. In such a situation, one would have expected simple mutilation of the cartouches and figures of the fallen monarch; instead, we find that the raised relief and hieroglyphic signs have been skimmed off the walls, leaving clearly readable scars. What we seem to have is a conscious attempt to remove from the tomb the magical 'machinery' that was intended to allow it to pass the dead king from this world to the next. It has been suggested that Amenmesse was in fact buried in this 'religionless' tomb: hopefully, the ongoing excavation of the sepulchre will enable us to test this theory.

Fig. 48. Quartzite statue bearing the names of King Sethos II; it is likely that this piece was originally made for Amenmesse, and formed a companion to the statue in fig. 45.

By the time Sethos II had regained power, he only had a year or two to live; he also now had a second wife, Tawosret, a lady of whose antecedents we are wholly ignorant. Work was resumed on his tomb (number KV 15 in the Valley of Kings), but both construction and decoration were far from completion when he breathed his last in the IV month of *Akhet* in his sixth year. Perhaps because of this, or maybe for other reasons, the mummy's interment, in the name of the new king, Siptah, took place in the tomb of Tawosret. It was to remain in her tomb for only a short while, however, being moved back to KV 15 when Tawosret's was taken over for the burial of Sethnakhte. Something over a century later, Sethos II's body was removed to a place of safety, ultimately finding rest in Amenophis II's tomb until moved to the Cairo Museum in the early twentieth century.

Siptah and Tawosret

c. 1195-1187 BC

The key figure in the days immediately following the death of Sethos II was the Chancellor Bay, apparently a man of Syrian origin, with the 'loyalist' surname, Ramesse-khaemnetjeru. Crown Prince Sethy-Merenptah B was either dead, or unable to assert his rights, for, as Bay himself proclaims, the Chancellor was able to 'establish the (new) king in the seat of his father': that father was none other than the late Amenmesse.

The new king, Siptah, was only in his early 'teens, and thus in need of a regency. In spite of his power, as a commoner, Bay could not aspire to such a role, but an obvious candidate was available in the form of the newly-widowed Great Royal Wife, Tawosret. The triumvirate thus established is made concrete at one end of the Valley of the Kings, where the three protagonists' tombs lie within yards of each other.

As can be seen from his mummy, the king suffered from a deformed left leg, his foot being forced into a vertical position by a shortened achilles tendon. This has been diagnosed as being as a result of polio, but is far more likely to have been a congenital defect, probably caused by cerebral palsy. At the beginning of the reign, he used the name Ramesses-Siptah, but for some reason rapidly altered it to Merenptah-Siptah, also changing his pre-nomen at the same time.

A modest number of monuments of the pharaoh are known from Memphis, Thebes and Nubia, one of the most remarkable, and of uncertain provenance, being a statue which showed Siptah on the lap of, probably, Amenmesse. The latter's figure was sub-sequently removed, presumably after Siptah's death.

For the first years of the reign, Tawosret's role was that of a conventional regent, rule being wholly in the name of the youthful Siptah. In perhaps the fifth year, however, a radical change took place, when Tawosret imitated that other queen-regent, Hatshepsut, in assuming full pharaonic titles. Work was immediately begun on constructing a new, 'king-size', burial hall in her tomb. In this, she planned to instal a fine semi-anthropoid granite coffin/sarcophagus, which was ultimately used for the interment of a Twentieth Dynasty prince elsewhere.

Work on this new burial chamber stopped, however, in II *Akhet* of Year 6. This date also seems to approximate to the demise of King Siptah. He may have been buried in his tomb, but without a name, for all cartouches seem to have been erased, although later restored. In Tawosret's neighbouring sepulchre, in which he had been represented with the queen, his names were swiftly altered to those of the late Sethos II.

The following two years of Tawosret's sole rule are little known. She greatly extended her tomb to full pharaonic dimen-sions, with a new, kingly, sarcophagus, and founded a mortuary temple on the Theban West Bank, the former largely complete at the time of her death or disappearance. It seems likely that her tenure of power was racked by dissention which may have grown into a full-scale civil war, in which the Chancellor Bay was one protagonist.

Another participant was a certain Sethnakhte, who would eventually emerge as victor. However, for a brief period, Bay seems to have reasserted his position, although the only identifiable action of his regime would appear to have been replacement of the erased cartouches in the tomb of his erstwhile protege, Siptah. His role was remembered, however, the Chancellor finding a place in the incoming dynasty's demonology as 'The Upstart Syrian'. Then he himself disappears from the scene; it seems unlikely that his royally-proportioned tomb in the Valley of the Kings was ever used for him, being found containing the burials of two later princes, one of them in the former sarcophagus of Regent Tawosret.

XIII   Defender of the Frontiers

Ramesses III

c. 1185-1153 BC

The origins of Sethnakhte, founder of the Twentieth Dynasty, are obscure. His name's compounding with that of the god Seth would suggest familial links with the Nineteenth Dynasty royal family, whose devotion to Seth is shown by the currency of the otherwise-unusual name, Sethy. Most probably, he was a grandson of Ramesses II by one of the latter's numerous offspring.

Sethnakhte was probably past middle-age when he took power from the regimes of Tawosret and Bay; certainly, his reign was extremely short, only the first two and a half passages of his tomb (KV 11) having been cut and partially decorated on his death. The king was accordingly buried in the tomb of Tawosret, the figures of the female pharaoh being covered in plaster and replaced by large writings of Sethnakhte's cartouches.

The old king was followed on the throne by his son, Ramesses III, who may have briefly served as his father's coregent. A rock-chapel near Deir el-Medina was dedicated in the kings' joint names, with another, already appropriated by Sethos II from Amenmesse, altered to bear Sethnakhte's cartouche.

The earliest years of the new reign were probably taken up with repairing the damage of the late-Nineteenth Dynasty conflicts, but by Ramesses III's fifth year, external threats had emerged that would test the mettle of the man who would prove to be the last truly great pharaoh. The first came from the west; Merenptah had had to repulse an attack by various Libyan tribes some twenty-seven years previously: now they made a new advance on the western Delta, ostensibly in response to Egyptian

142

Fig. 49. King Ramesses III offering maet *('truth') to Amun-Re (temple of Karnak).*

interference in their internal politics. In the battle that followed, Ramesses' forces were wholly successful: thousands of the enemy were killed, and many more captured. Nevertheless, the Libyan population of the western Delta continued to increase by peaceful infiltration, and would later form the basis for a line that would ultimately take the throne of Egypt. The second, far more serious, threat came three years later:

> The foreign countries conspired in their islands, and the lands were dislodged and scattered in battle together; no land could stand before their arms: the land of the Hittites, Qode, Carchemesh, Arzawa and Cyprus were wasted, and they set up a camp in southern Syria. They desolated its people and made its land as if non-existent. They bore fire before them as they came forward towards Egypt.

The confederacy which had thus liquidated the principal states of Syria and Asia Minor comprised a number of separate peoples, perhaps originally driven from their homelands by famine and tempted by the promise of the rich lands to the east.

Most came from the Aegean, which had recently experienced the collapse of the main centres of the Mycenaean civilization, together with the decay of the western part of the Hittite Empire, including such places as Troy. Thus released from central control, the various islands and coastal polities became 'loose cannon' in the international arena which had long been regulated by such treaties as that between Ramesses II and Hattusilis III.

Of their destruction of the great Hittite monarchy, and the ancient states of Syria we have a number of contemporary accounts, telling of attacks from land and sea that destroyed much of the civilization of the Late Bronze Age. From their base in Syria, the main fighting units of the invaders, now known as the 'Sea Peoples', proceeded south by ship, with their families and support elements following by land, transported by ox-carts.

To face these invaders, Ramesses III established a defensive line in southern Palestine, with the mouths of the Nile secured by squadrons of warships and merchantmen. Commanding the land-forces himself, he succeeded in signally defeating the opposition, while the sea-battle in and around the Delta resulted in an overwhelming Egyptian victory. Elements of the enemy, in particular the Philistines, were able to settle in Palestine, but their power was entirely broken, and Egypt safe on the eastern frontier. It is possible that the victory was followed up by an expedition into Syria-Palestine, to mop up opposition and reinforce the Egyptian presence in the area. Amongst the memorials of the war against the Sea Peoples was a great structure was built at Medinet Habu, which in all essentials imitates the features of a Syrian fortress, or *migdol*.

Regnal year 11, however, saw yet another invasion from Libya. Again, the enemy was driven back, over 2,000 men being killed, and the captured leaders executed. While this seems to have brought peace for the rest of the reign, problems persisted throughout the dynasty, although more in the form of incursions from the desert around the latitude of Thebes than direct attacks on the Delta. Other, more desirable, foreign contacts took place, however, in particular a re-establishment of contacts with Egypt's old trading partner, Punt.

With the coming of peace, after six or more years of conflict, a major programme of building was begun, supplemented by another of tree-planting and a consolidation of law and order. At Karnak, the High Priesthood had been since the beginning of the dynasty held by Bakenkhonsu ii, son of the General Amenémopet, followed in the twenties of Ramesses III's reign by Usermaetrenakhte, who was to remain in office until around the time of the king's death. The temple-buildings there were augmented by numerous reliefs and two new, small temples founded, one dedicated to the moon-god, Khonsu. Other Egyptian centres also benefited from the king's constructional works, including Piramesse, Athribis, Heliopolis, Memphis, Ashmunein, Asyut, Abydos and Edfu.

The vizierate, for many generations split between Upper and Lower Egypt, was unified in the person of To, possibly as a result of the rebellion of an unnamed Lower Egyptian vizier during the reign. A number of major offices were assigned to the king's sons.

Fig. 50. Osiride figures of Ramesses III in the forecourt of his small temple at Karnak..

145

It is very clear that Ramesses III was a great devotee of Ramesses II: not only was his prenomen based on that of his ancestor, but his sons were named after those of the earlier king, and often received the same offices as their namesakes. A particular example of this is Khaemwaset C, who became *sem*-priest of Ptah at Memphis, just as had the famous prince of earlier times, although he never rose to the dignity of High Priest.

Ramesses III had two principal wives; one remains anonymous, but the other was Iset B, who was the mother of the king's eldest surviving sons, Generalissimo Ramesse C, and the Master of Horse, Amenhirkopshef C. A number of older boys died during their father's reign, and were buried in the Valley of the Queens. Of younger offspring who survived at the end of the reign, two of the most important were the Master of Horse, Sethhirkopshef C, and the High Priest of Re at Heliopolis, Meryatum B.

In addition to these individuals, Ramesses III possessed a number of minor wives and their offspring, and in this lay the seeds of the end of his reign – and life. The late twenties saw economic problems that are most visible in the failures to pay the Deir el-Medina workmen that led to a sit-down strike by them in year 29. Against this background was hatched a plot against the king's life, with the aim of placing on the throne the Prince Pentaweret, born of one Tiye, setting aside the rightful heir, Ramesse C.

The insurrection had a number of facets; in addition to the murder of the king, a popular rebellion was to be stirred up, with a magical element that involved the use of waxen images. Only one of these succeeded however: the murder of the king. The remainder were rapidly squashed by loyalists, and a tribunal set up by the new king, Ramesses IV, to try the conspirators, all of whom were condemned to take their own lives, as a mark of their rank.

Ramesses III was buried in his huge tomb in the Valley of the Kings. It had been constructed out of the unfinished beginning of Sethnakhte's sepulchre, and is interesting in incorporating a number of sculpted scenes that are unique for a royal tomb. The royal mortuary temple lay at Medinet Habu, and was in many ways a copy of that of Ramesses II, the Ramesseum. It is the best preserved of all New Kingdom mortuary structures, and was for many years the headquarters of the Theban necropolis administration.

The interment of the third Ramesses marks the end of an era in Egyptian history. Although the royal line was to continue, the vitality of the New Kingdom was all but spent, and never again would Egypt occupy such a lofty position on the world stage as it had done under the Tuthmosides and earlier Ramessides. The reasons are various; firstly, the technical revolution of the Iron Age, beginning around 1200 BC, left Egypt behind, lacking as she did easily-exploitable sources of ore. Secondly, however, the civil wars of the late Nineteenth Dynasty had fatally fractured the join between northern Egypt and that portion centred on the Thebaid. The leitmotif for much of the rest of Egyptian history is the overt or covert conflict between the two portions of the country, frustrating any further attempts at truly national action.

XIV Of Kings and Priests

Ramesses IV, V, VI, VII, VIII and IX

c. 1153-1104 BC

As Crown Prince, Ramesses IV seems to have taken an increasingly important role in the rule of Egypt during the closing years of his father's reign. For example, as early as year 27, he is depicted as being responsible for the appointment of one Amenemopet as High Priest of Mut at Karnak in the latter's tomb on Dira Abu'l-Naga at Western Thebes. The conspiracy that ended Ramesses III's life and reign was doubtless aimed as much against Prince Ramesses as his father: the vigour with which the new king saw to the punishment of the conspirators and the commemoration of the late king in the Great Harris Papyrus is not surprising. The latter document is a listing of the third Ramesses' good works, in particular donations to his own divine cult, and is one of the largest papyrus documents to survive.

In his own right, Ramesses IV pushed ahead with plans for new buildings. Extensive quarrying for greywacke took place in the Wadi Hammamat, most probably for his huge mortuary temple, a building that was never to be completed. Early in his reign, Ramesses IV changed his prenomen from *User*maetre-setpenamun to *Heqa*maetre-setpenamun; this was presumably intended to avoid popular confusion with the prenomina of Ramesses II and III, respectively Usermaetre-setpenre and Usermaetre-meryamun.

There is some slender evidence for some sea-borne conflict in Ramesses IV's third year, perhaps the outcome of a final thrust on the part of the Sea Peoples. In the south, Nubia was ruled by Hori ii, son of a namesake who had been viceroy since Siptah's time, and who would continue in office until Ramesses VI's reign. Other-

Fig. 51. *King Ramesses IV is given 'life' by Re (temple of Khonsu at Karnak).*

wise, there is little evidence for Ramesses IV's activities outside Egypt-proper.

The vizierate, under Neferrenpet, seems to have remained unified. The incumbent is known to have travelled around the country fairly extensively, and was involved in the choice of the site for the royal tomb, KV 2 in the Valley of the Kings. It was a sepulchre that the king was to occupy all too soon: in a stela from Abydos, Ramesses IV prayed that he might be allowed the span of Ramesses II; regrettably, his sixth regnal year was his last.

Likewise short was the reign of his son, Ramesses V Amenhirkopshef I, cut off by what appears to have been smallpox. Since Ramesses V died without surviving issue, the throne accordingly reverted to Ramesses IV's younger brother, Prince Amenhirkopshef C, known today as Ramesses VI Amenhirkopshef II. The new king took over Ramesses V's tomb for himself, apparently burying his predecessor in another sepulchre, after around a year's delay. The sixth Ramesses is the last known king to have worked the turquoise mines of the Sinai, and although a number of martial statues are known, together with a Karnak relief, there is no certain evidence of his foreign policy.

Dynastic misfortune struck again only a few years after Ramesses VI's death, as his son and successor, Itamun (Ramesses VII) lost his own son, Ramesse, prematurely. He was thus followed by yet another son of Ramesses III, Sethhirkopshef C (Ramesses VIII), whose brief tenure was followed by the reign of his nephew, Khaemwaset (D), probably the son of Montjuhirkopshef B, a junior offspring of Ramesses III.

As Ramesses IX Khaemwaset I, he reigned for nineteen years. These were marked by various problems, economic ones being illustrated by the massive increases in grain prices seen

Fig. 52. Statuette from Karnak, originally made for Ramesses V, showing the king presenting a figure of Amun-Re. It was later usurped by his uncle, Ramesses VI, who added crude inscriptions, including figures of his mother, Iset-Tahemdjeret, and his son, Panebenkemyt, the latter being visible in this view.

during the reigns of Ramesses VII through XI. The resulting lawlessness is manifested in large-scale looting in the Theban necropolis; amongst the most interesting documents to survive from ancient times are the transcripts of the trials of a number of persons accused of plundering both royal and private tombs.

A fair few monuments survive from his reign, both in the Nile valley and out at Dakhla Oasis. At Heliopolis, his son Nebmaetre, named after Ramesses VI's prenomen, held the High Priesthood, while, initially, Ramessenakhte continued in the office of High Priest of Amun, which he had held since the beginning of Ramesses IV's reign. Soon, however, he was replaced by Nesamun, whose tenure, however, was to be short-lived; by year 10, one Amunhotpe was in office. In a set of reliefs at Karnak, the priest is most remarkably shown on the same scale as his king – an unheard-of presumption: even such a powerful figure as Horemheb had been shown as a being a small fraction of the height of the young Tutankhamun. This was to be a flavour of things to come.

Ramesses IX was buried in the Valley of the Kings, as was his son, Montjuhirkopshef C, perhaps his original heir. The king's mummy was found at Deir el-Bahari, and is the latest extant body of a New Kingdom monarch known to survive.

Ramesses X and XI

c. 1104-1064 BC

Nothing is certainly known of Ramesses X Amenhirkopshef III's relationship to his predecessors, although it is usually assumed that he was a son of Ramesses IX. His reign was fairly short, and has few attestations, while the king's tomb (KV 18) was barely begun. Ramesses X was followed by the last king of the Twentieth Dynasty line, Ramesses XI Khaemwaset II – presumably his son. Like his predecessor, the new ruler's monuments are few and far between, but there is clear evidence for some fairly dramatic events during his reign's final decade.

Since the time of Ramesses IX, when Amunhotpe had assumed the pontificate, the temporal power and prestige of the High

Priesthood of Amun had been increasing. Whether or not related to this inflated status, the reign of Ramesses X or XI saw a nine-month period when Amunhotpe was 'suppressed', clearly as part of some kind of major civil upheaval, which included an attack on the fortified temple-complex of Medinet Habu.

These troubles were ultimately brought to a conclusion by the Viceroy of Nubia, Panehsy, marching north to Thebes to restore order. For possibly a period of years he held sway over both southern Egypt and Nubia, until he perhaps overreached himself and had to be removed by the General Piankh. Panehsy was driven into Nubia; he seems to have survived there, and it was perhaps his heirs, or those of his associates, who were to be responsible for establishing a new Nubian monarchy, whose later scions we shall be meeting later as conquerors of Egypt.

For his part in the war, Piankh additionally received the office of High Priest of Amun from the king. He thus acquired the authority of effective military dictator of much of Upper Egypt. On his death shortly afterwards, this authority was acquired by one Hrihor, who married Piankh's widow, Nodjmet. Within a short while, he had arrogated quasi-royal status, beginning to use cartouches for his work within the temple of Khonsu at Karnak. The regime of Piankh had marked its establishment by the institution of a new dating era, known as the 'Repeating of Births', starting in a 'year 1', corresponding to the nineteenth regnal year of Ramesses XI. It continued for the remainder of the latter's reign, whose end seems to have closely corresponded with the death of Hrihor as well; this saw the latter's replacement in all his offices bar his 'kingship' by his step-son, the son of Piankh, Pinudjem I.

Ramesses XI had spent the majority of his reign away from Thebes, presumably resident in the north. The lack of royal contact with the southern city and the disruption of the past years is shown by the state of Ramesses XI's tomb, undecorated after its owner had spent nearly three decades on the throne. This diminution of royal power even in the Delta is shown by the position of Smendes, probably the brother of Nodjmet, who had married a daughter of Ramesses XI, as governor of the northern outlier of Piramesse, Tanis. In the report of one Wenamun, sent by Hrihor on an expedition to the Lebanon, he notes presenting

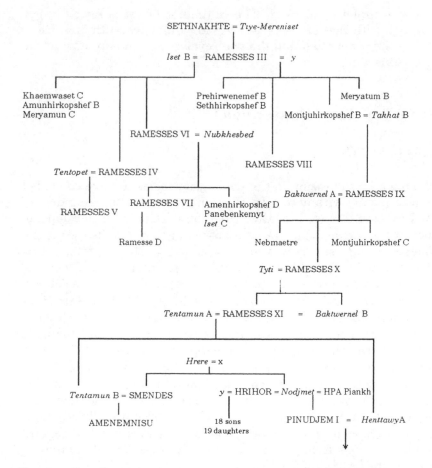

Fig. 53. Genealogical table for the Twentieth Dynasty and the beginning of the Twenty-first .

his credentials to Smendes and his wife, Tentamun, but is wholly silent as regards his nominal king, Ramesses XI, possibly resident only a few kilometres distant. On the last Ramesside's death, it was his son- in-law Smendes who would succeed him as pharaoh.

Apart from Ramesses XI, who was clearly never buried in his intended Theban tomb, all the Ramesside kings seem to have been buried in the Valley of the Kings, although the sepulchre of Ramesses VIII remains unidentified, and that of Ramesses X almost completely blocked. The mummies of these latter kings, together with that of Ramesses VII are unknown, although those of the others were found in the two royal caches and are now in the Cairo Museum.

Pinudjem I and Psusennes I

c.1049-981 BC

Pinudjem I's succession to the pontificate seems to have coincided almost exactly with accession of his maternal uncle, Smendes, to the Egyptian throne. The latter ruled from Tanis, a former dependency of Piramesse, which was fast becoming a city in its own right. The new king's status was acknowledged in Thebes, which now abandoned the 'Repeating of Births' system in favour of Smendes' regnal years. However, the effective independence of the soldier-priests was clearly established: revealingly, Theban date-lines never actually name the Tanite king whose regnal year they quote.

The Thebans' writ seems to have run from north of El-Hiba to the southern frontier, which, following the expulsion of Panehsy, seems to have lain a relatively short distance into Nubia. To the north lay the *de facto* (as against *de joure*) realm of the pharaoh, including the old capital of Memphis, but centred on the new delta capital of Tanis. As head of the Theban regime, Pinudjem is known to have been active in protecting the royal mummies, still seriously at risk from plunderers, as well as considerable building work at the fortress of El-Hiba.

As far as one can tell, the division of Egypt seems to have worked fairly well – certainly there are no surviving indications of conflict. A major upheaval of Tanite-Theban relations occurred, however, around year 16 of Smendes. For a period of time, although claiming no more than his military-priestly titles, Pinudjem had executed a number of monuments showing him in full pharaonic regalia. Although in one case a representation was altered back to showing him in priestly garb, as if to hint at some hesitation on Pinudjem's part, from year 16 we find him bearing full pharaonic titles. While the first of the Theban soldier-priests,

Fig. 54. Colossal statue bearing the names of Pinudjem I in front of the second pylon at Karnak. It also bears the names of Ramesses II and there remains controversy as to whether it was carved for Pinudjem out of a monument of the earlier king, or was simply usurped by him.

Hrihor, had used kingly titles, they are only found within the temple setting and are never referred to by his descendants, while his prenomen was simply 'Hemnetjertepyenamun' – 'High Priest of Amun'. In contrast, Pinudjem I used a proper prenomen, and clearly retained his dignity in the minds of posterity. Only in his dating did he fail to show total independence, continuing to use the years of Smendes, whose co-regent he now was.

A further indication of his 'proper' kingship was the fact that his high priesthood was passed on to his son Masaharta while Pinudjem yet lived. Shown by his mummy to have been a man of considerable girth, Masaharta is known from a set of sphinxes in the Great Temple at Karnak, and marked linen from contemporary mummy-wrappings. He established himself at the Theban regime's major headquarters at El-Hiba, and it was there that he seems to have fallen ill and died around year 24, after less than a decade as High Priest and Generalissimo.

The appointment of a fresh soldier-pontiff appears to have been followed by a major outbreak of trouble in Thebes. The new man, Djedkhonsuefankh, was another of Pinudjem's sons, but his term of office was momentary. It is conceivable that he died by violence in the events that led to his younger brother, Menkheper-re, assuming the priesthood in year 25 and proceeding southward to Thebes to 'pacify the land and suppress his enemy'. As recorded on a stela, a number of those implicated in the troubles were exiled to the western oases, to be recalled a few years later, perhaps as part of Menkheperre's final settlement of the difficulties within the Thebaid. This recall of exiles occurred in the reign of a successor of Smendes who had now died in the twenty-sixth year of his reign, and was apparently buried at Tanis. His immediate successor was his son(?) Amenemnisu, but by the end of his apparent four-year *florouit*, King Amenemnisu was sharing the Tanite throne with another: Psusennes I.

With Psusennes' accession, the line of Piankh had finally obtained control of the whole of Egypt, for Psusennes was almost certainly the son of Pinudjem I, by his wife, Henttawy, probably the daughter of Ramesses XI; through this link, we occasionally find the king writing out his name in full as Ramesses-Psusennes. Definite monuments away from Tanis are few, the most important being a chapel to Isis, connected with the pyramid of a wife of Kheops. However, Psusennes was apparently the ruler responsible for turning Tanis into a fully-fledged capital city, surrounding its temple with a huge brick *temenos* wall, the sanctuary, dedicated to Amun, being largely composed of blocks salvaged from the now-derelict Piramesse. Many of these bore the names of the latter city's builder, Ramesses II, including obelisks, re-erected without textual modification. Through their presence at the site, Tanis was long misidentified as the former Piramesse and Avaris. Amongst Psusennes' buildings was one built jointly with his father, now clearly a very old man.

Pinudjem I died some time after year 7 of Psusennes I, and was buried at Thebes in a coffin that had once belonged to Tuthmosis I. This antique piece, presumably salvaged from Tuthmosis' robbed tomb in the Valley of the Kings, was extensively re-worked, with rich gilding and inlay. Pinudjem's adoption of this four hundred and fifty year old case may not have been fortuitous, since there is clear evidence for his interest in the Tuthmoside pharaohs. Not only did his son, Menkheperre, bear the name that had been the prenomen of the glorious Tuthmosis III, but his daughter, the God's Wife of Amun (head of the female clergy), was Maetkare: over four centuries earlier this name had adorned the prenomen-cartouche of none other than Hatshepsut herself.

There are indications that Pinudjem I had contemplated taking over the unfinished tomb of Ramesses XI for himself at the very beginning of his kingship. Little was done, however, and the actual tomb of Pinudjem I remains unidentified. Ultimately, the coffin and mummy came to rest in the Deir el-Bahari cache. Regrettably, the body's current location uncertain, possibly having lost its label during one of the Egyptian Museum's moves.

The brethren Psusennes I and Menkheperre were presumably of a similar age, for they were to hold their respective offices, essentially in parallel, for half a century. The soldier-priests continued their father's work on the fortifications of El-Hiba, also doing much to protect the sacred sites of Thebes from profane encroachment. Menkheperre's last attestation is in his brother's year 48, his death probably falling not long afterwards, the pontificate falling to his son, Smendes II.

Psusennes I had married his sister, Mutnodjmet, and the Lady Wiay. Only two of his children are certainly identifiable. A daughter, Isetemkheb C, married her uncle, Menkheperre, while a son was Ramesse-Ankhefenmut. The latter seems to have fallen into disgrace, to judge from the excision of his name from the inscriptions of his burial chamber.

A major figure at the Tanite court was the General Wendjeba-endjed, who besides his military and civil titles held a number that marked him out as a major figure in the king's religious organization. His status is shown by the unprecedented favour granted him of burial within the king's own tomb. Another man of prominence must have been Amenemopet, Psusennes' eventual successor; he is normally thought of as the old king's son, but no evidence survives. If so, he must have been born fairly early in Psusennes I's career, since he was himself of a fairly advanced age when the latter died, having spent his last years crippled by arthritis.

Psusennes I's tomb was built just outside the gateway of the Amun-temple at Tanis, comprising a number of chambers, built in a pit, and later covered over and probably surmounted by a funerary chapel of brick. Apart from Wendjebaendjed and the king himself, chambers were set aside for Mutnodjmet and Ankh-efenmut. Psusennes was buried wearing a mask of gold, covered with a chased sheet of gold, within a coffin of sold silver. This lay inside a granite coffin, taken over from a Theban worthy of the Nineteenth Dynasty, outside which was a magnificent granite sarco-phagus. The latter was also a second-hand piece, taken like his father's coffin from the far-away Valley of the Kings. It had originally served as the innermost of Merenptah's nest of three sarcophagi, the outer pair of which were demolished to allow its extraction.

The tomb was found by Pierre Montet in 1939, and proved to have escaped the attention of robbers. The damp conditions had destroyed almost all organic remains, but much splendid jewellery and other metalwork was recovered. The sadly decayed remains of the king's body lay for many years in the anatomy department of the Qasr el-Aini Hospital in Cairo.

XV   The Rise and Fall of the Libyan Pharaohs

Shoshenq I

c. 948-927 BC

Although it is generally assumed that Amenemopet, was Psusennes I's son, a clear break in the line of his dynasty appears to occur after the former's death. Amenemopet's successor was one Osorkon, the son of the Libyan Chief of the Ma, (Meshwesh), Shoshenq A, by the Lady Mehetweskhet. His existence was first established as recently as 1977. He is probably best referred to by the Greek form of his name, Osokhor, to avoid having to change the long-established numberings of the later Kings Osorkon.

The significance of this Libyan appearance on the Tanite throne is unclear; Libyans had been amongst the foes of Merenptah and Ramesses III, but there is no evidence of any kind of violent take-over. Rather, the family in question seem to have been resident in Egypt for generations, distinguished mainly by their ancestral names and titles. Indeed, it is possible that the line of Hrihor contained Libyan blood, since a number of its scions, from the Priest-General's sons, Osorkon, Masaqaharta, and Masaharta, to the latter's namesake, Pinudjem I's son and successor as High Priest of Amun, bore Libyan names.

Thus, what we may see is that Amenemopet's death was followed by the assumption of the crown by a collateral line of the existing family, with the senior members of the dynasty retaining the Upper Egyptian command, in the form of Menkheperre's sons, the High Priests Smendes II and Pinudjem II, and the latter's offspring and successor, Psusennes II.

Osokhor's reign was short, and was followed by that of Siamun, whose family links are unknown. His purely-Egyptian name need not count against such a filiation, as the aforementioned

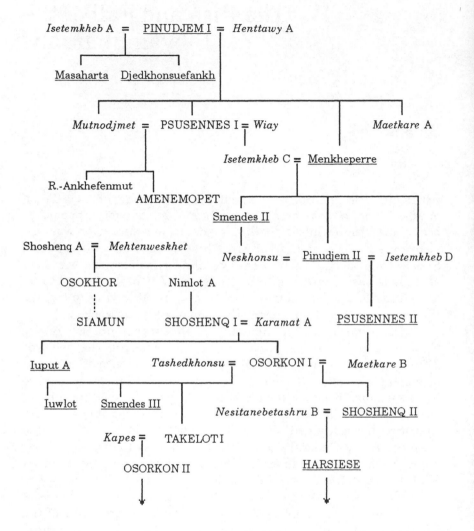

Fig. 55. Genealogical table for the Twenty-first and early Twenty-second Dynasties (High Priests of Amun are underlined).

family of Hrihor contained a mixture of name-types within a single generation; on the other hand, he may represent a member of the Theban branch taking back control after Osokhor's death without male issue. Siamun's reign was particularly marked by an increase in the activities of the Theban regime in rescuing the ancient royal mummies from the depredations of the tomb robbers, which were now gathered together in two or three distinct groups, in and outside the Valley of the Kings.

It is not wholly certain what happened directly after Siamun's death. The High Priest Psusennes II is known to have assumed full royal names and titles, but it is unclear whether he did so as Siamun's successor as Tanite king, or merely as a junior co-regent, in the same way Pinudjem I had been. The latter seems the more likely, in which case Siamun was followed on the throne by the former Chief of the Ma, Shoshenq B, the nephew of the late King Osokhor, and now the founder of the Twenty-second Dynasty. Indeed, it is possible that Shoshenq had acquired quasi-pharaonic power while Siamun yet lived, since a text from Karnak names him as only a Chieftain, but also gives him a second regnal year.

While yet Chief of the Ma, possibly based at Bubastis in the south-eastern Delta, Shoshenq I had petitioned the god Amun for the establishment of an Abydene cenotaph for his father, Nimlot A, as recorded on a stela from that city. As king himself, he now undertook to restore the authority of the monarchy, with an ending of the system by which the south had enjoyed effective independence under its line of soldier-priests. The elevation of Psusennes II to nominal kingship may have been a painless way to remove the old line from its entrenched place in Thebes, combined with the marriage of Shoshenq's son and heir, Osorkon, to Psusennes daughter, Maetkare B. The Libyan king was thus enabled to install his own son, Iuput, as High Priest of Amun, the parental link discouraging the new pontiff from attempting to continue the south's independence; nevertheless, Iuput continued the old tradition of linking his priestly office with arguably the more significant office of Army-Leader, and later Governor of Upper Egypt.

Amongst Iuput's duties in Thebes was the safeguarding of the royal mummies that had for years been fighting a losing battle against the omnipresent tomb-robber. One group of bodies had long since reached their final destination, the tomb of Amenophis II in the Valley of the Kings; another, of considerably greater size, was, some time after Shoshenq I's eleventh year, moved from their earlier hiding-place(s) to a large gallery just south of Deir el-Bahari (TT 320), which had a few years earlier been adapted as the tomb of the late High Priest Pinudjem II and his immediate family. There, the mummies remained until rediscovered by modern plunderers in AD 1871.

Another son of the king, Nimlot B, was appointed as a military governor, based at Herakleopolis. At Memphis, the High Priesthood continued to be held by the incumbent family, in the person of Shedsunefertum A, who also held the distinction of being a king's brother-in-law, having married a daughter of a ruler of the Twenty-first Dynasty.

Apart from the possibility of some activity by Siamun, there is no real evidence for Egyptian military intervention in Palestine from the late Ramesside period until the reign of Shoshenq I. By then, he doubtless felt secure in his control of Egypt: his sons controlled the Nile valley, and a minor disturbance out at Dakhla Oasis had been cleared by the king's emissary, Wayheset. Accordingly, Shoshenq prepared to embark on the first large-scale north-eastern campaigns by Egyptian armies for two centuries.

Two separate incursions seem to have been made. One is recorded in a commemorative inscription in the temple of Karnak and penetrated at least as far north as Megiddo, where a stela was erected. For the other campaign, our only source is the Old Testament *First Book of Kings*:

> In the fifth year of King Rehoboam, ... Shishak (i.e. Shoshenq), King of Egypt, came up against Jerusalem. He took away the treasures of the House of Yahweh, and the treasures of the house of the king: he took all. He took all the golden shields that Solomon had made.

At the end of his reign, Shoshenq was embarking on a large-scale building programme within the Karnak complex, ordering extensive sandstone quarrying at Gebel Silsila to provide for it. This comprised a huge new forecourt, a gateway in its south-east corner, known today as the 'Bubastite Portal', being adorned with scenes of the king and the High Priest Iuput receiving the favours of the gods.

162

Fig. 56. The Bubastite Portal, built in the south-east corner of the First Court of the temple of Karnak to commemorate the exploits of King Shoshenq I.

The exterior walls were clearly intended to bear depictions of Shoshenq I's military prowess, but only one scene was actually carved, depicting the first(?) of his Palestinian campaigns. However, nothing else was ever done, as shortly afterwards the king died. His burial place is uncertain, since, although the last kings of the Twenty-first Dynasty had been interred in the same Tanite necropolis as their predecessors, the earliest use of that particular area by a Twenty-second Dynasty king is by Osorkon II, a hundred years after Shoshenq I's death. It is possible that he might have been buried elsewhere at Tanis, or even at his natal town of Bubastis, but there is no real evidence available.

One item of his funerary equipment has, however, come to light, albeit via the antiquities market, without any information as to its place of origin. This is his canopic chest, now in Berlin; of alabaster, it is wholly unlike the wooden examples of other kings of the period, and seems to be an approximate copy of a king's chest of Eighteenth or Nineteenth Dynasty date. The possession of such an item fits well with the New Kingdom-style military ambition displayed by Shoshenq's Palestinian campaign – an ambition that does not seem to have been shared by his successors.

Osorkon II and Harsiese

c. 877-838 BC

On Shoshenq I's death, the throne passed to Osorkon I. Soon after his accession, the new king's brother, Iuput, died, was buried in a large granite-lined tomb at Abydos, and was succeeded as High Priest of Amun by Osorkon I's eldest son, Shoshenq C. Born of Queen Maetkare, his was accordingly the heritage of both the current dynasty, and the old line of Theban High Priests. Towards the end of Osorkon I's long reign, Shoshenq, now in his fifties, became his father's co-regent, and was replaced as pontiff by a brother, Iuwlot. Unfortunately, Shoshenq II died shortly afterwards, as a result of an infected head-wound, leaving a son, Harsiese.

When Osorkon I himself died soon afterwards, he was followed by Takelot I, a son by the Lady Kapes. The reign of Takelot I is particularly obscure. Thebes continued to be ruled by the High Priest Iuwlot, and then by his brother, Smendes III, but hardly anything else is known of the events of Takelot I's occupation of the throne. He was buried at Tanis, the final interment being carried out by his son, in a Middle Kingdom sarcophagus, in a redecorated chamber of a tomb that had probably once belonged to King Smendes.

Takelot I's son was Osorkon II, probably a young man at his accession, given that his reign was to last for nearly forty years. Probably one of his first actions was to appoint a new High Priest of Amun – if this had not already been done by his father. Rather than a son or brother of the reigning king, the man chosen was none other than Harsiese, the son of Shoshenq II.

This selection may be seen as unwise: a son or brother of a king would usually have a sufficient stake in the dynasty to remain loyal, but Harsiese's position was different. Had Shoshenq II lived, Harsiese would have become pharaoh in due course; as it was, he was on a collateral line, and possibly nursed some bitterness about his fate. Moreover, as the great-grandson of Psusennes II, as well as Shoshenq I, he may have felt that he possessed blood royal of a rather purer nature than his cousin, Osorkon II.

The outcome, a decade or so later, was fairly inevitable. After seventy or eighty years during which Thebes had become once more under the close authority of the crown, the High Priest did as Pinudjem I had done, and obtained full pharaonic titles, while passing the pontificate itself to a son. Harsiese henceforth remained at the head of the Thebaid until his death, although latterly incapacitated by illness. His tomb lay within the *temenos* of the temples of Medinet Habu, and revealed his skull. This contains a hole, apparently made through a surgical procedure which the king seems to have survived, to judge from the healing shown by the wound. The priest-king had been buried in the trough of a granite coffin taken from the tomb of Ramesses II's sister, Henutmire, closed by a lid which bore the head of a falcon. This remarkable coffin-form was usual in royal burials of the Twenty-second Dynasty, and symbolised amongst other things the king's status as an incarnation of the falcon-god, Horus.

Elsewhere in Egypt, however, the practice of installing royal sons in positions of power was continued from previous reigns, and extended at Memphis, where the old-established line of High Priests was supplanted by the Crown Prince Shoshenq D, born to Osorkon II by Queen Karomat B. The approach was also re-adopted at Thebes after the end of the pontificate of Harsiese's son, when Prince Nimlot C became High Priest of Amun. It is possible that Harsiese's son may have been cut off prematurely, because his name has been largely removed from his only certain monument. Nimlot combined his High Priesthood with his earlier post, the governorship of Herakleopolis and Middle Egypt, in which he followed his earlier namesake, the son of Shoshenq I. Nimlot C predeceased his father, Osorkon II, being followed in the pontif-

Fig. 57. Osorkon II, from his jubilee hall in the temple at Bubastis.

icate by his own son, Takelot F. The female side of the Amun clergy was headed by the God's Wife, Karomat G; she was certainly a king's daughter, but the identity of her father is uncertain – presumably either Takelot I, Osorkon II or Harsiese.

Another son of Osorkon II to gain a High Priestly title was the young Harnakhte. His 'living' was the cult of Amun at Tanis, the royal capital; that his role was purely nominal is shown by his death while still a child of 8 or 9. The temple of Amun in the city had been begun by Psusennes I, and a court added by Siamun. Osorkon II was responsible for the construction of a new forecourt, and other outlying structures; as with most of the material used in the construction of Tanis, much of the stonework derived from the demolition of Piramesse. Another Delta city that benefited from Osorkon II's attentions was Bubastis, where major additions were made to the temple of the cat-goddess, Bastet, again reusing elements from constructions of Ramesses II.

At least part of the work at Bubastis was connected with the king's celebration of his jubilee in year 22: it is, as usual in such cases, unknown why he deviated from the normal thirty-year threshold for holding such a festival. A year later, an Apis bull was buried at Saqqara by the High Priest, Prince Shoshenq D, but within a few years, the heir to the throne was himself dead, and buried in a tomb within the temple of Ptah at Memphis. He was succeeded by his son, Takelot B.

Osorkon II did little to imitate his great-grandfather, Shoshenq I, in the area of foreign relations. A statue was presented to the ruler of Egypt's old friend, Byblos, and the remains of a vase from Samaria seem to attest to some contacts with the Kingdom of Israel. However, the limit to Osorkon's physical involvement would appear to have been a thousand troops contributed to the coalition of Syro-Palestinian polities that opposed the Assyrian king, Shalmaneser III (c. 859-824 BC), at the Battle of Qarqar in 853. The very last years of Osorkon II's reign saw an alternative approach taken: gifts of various exotic fauna were sent to the Assyrian king, which the latter was happy to present as 'tribute' from Egypt.

Little else is known of the remaining fifteen years of Osorkon II's reign, except that, possibly encouraged by the Tanite king's advancing age, Thebes made another stab at independence. Thus, Osorkon's last two years saw him sharing the pharaonic dignity with a certain Takelot II of Thebes, effectively marking the end of Egypt as a unitary state for a period of nearly two centuries. That this split was rapidly recognized abroad is suggested by the mention of 'kings of Egypt' in a Biblical passage that refers to this very period.

When Osorkon II died, he was buried at Tanis in the tomb he had earlier appropriated for himself and his late father, now numbered NRT I. He was interred in a gigantic sarcophagus, its lid carved from the remains of a group-statue of the Ramesside Period. The burial chamber was shared with his young son, Harnakhte, whose tenure as the local pontiff of Amun had proved to be sadly short-lived. The tomb was robbed in antiquity, only a few fragments, including debris of the hawk-headed coffin, and the canopic jars being certainly identifiable from Osorkon's burial.

Shoshenq III

c.838-798 BC

At Tanis, Osorkon II was succeeded by Shoshenq III, presumably his son, although no certain evidence survives. Since he bore the same name as the late Crown Prince, Shoshenq D, it is possible that he may have been born after the latter's death, making him but a teenager at accession; this would certainly fit in with Shoshenq III's forty-year reign.

The king married the Lady Tentamenopet; he had three known sons, his prematurely-deceased heir, Bakennefi, Pashedbast, and his second successor, Pimay. Another son may have been the Shoshenq who seems to have followed Shoshenq III as the fourth pharaoh of the name.

Shoshenq III's authority was acknowledged by the great array of 'princedoms' and 'chiefdoms' which had sprung up throughout the Delta during the middle of the Twenty-second Dynasty. Based on each of the major cities of the area, this network of territories was to remain a key element of Egyptian politics for the remainder of pharaonic history. Some of them were held by members of the royal house, but others were held by hereditary lines that were seemingly self-perpetuating. Even more than the detachment of Thebes, the growth of the Delta princedoms marked the beginning of the end of the old Egypt.

Shoshenq III was a considerable builder at his capital, as usual employing recycled earlier monuments as raw material. This was as true of his pylon to the temple of Amun-Re as of his sarcophagus, the latter in origin a lintel of two Thirteenth Dynasty kings. At Memphis he built a chapel, similar monuments also being constructed at a number of Delta sites. Also datable to Shoshenq's reign is an Apis burial, and the interment of the High Priest of Ptah, Takelot B in a tomb near that of the latter's father, Shoshenq D.

In spite of the number of local rulers who were in existence by the latter part of his reign, Shoshenq III's position as nominal overlord of all of Egypt does not seem to have been seriously challenged. After four decades on the throne, he was interred in

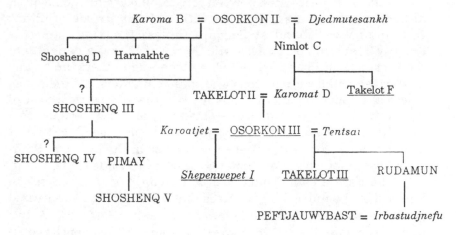

Fig. 58. Genealogical table for the later Twenty-second and Theban Twenty-third Dynasty.

tomb NRT V at Tanis, the burial presumably being conducted by the new king, Shoshenq IV, whose reign was so unremarkable that his very existence was only first noticed in the late 1980s.

Takelot II, Pedubast I and Osorkon III

c. 841-769 BC

When he inherited his northern throne, Shoshenq III seems also inherited a king in Thebes, of the 'Theban Twenty-third Dynasty', which can be regarded as having been initiated with the assumption of royal style by Harsiese some decades before. For many years, Takelot II was regarded as a member of the Tanite royal line, but a growing number of scholars now believe that he actually ruled at Thebes only, in parallel with the Twenty-second Dynasty line.

We are wholly ignorant of Takelot II's antecedents, although he may have been none other than the High Priest Takelot F, whose term of office would seem to have come to an end at around the time of Takelot II's assumption of the Theban kingship.

169

Takelot II's activities were largely confined to his home area, although a block naming him with a High Priest of Ptah, Merenptah, was found at Saqqara (unless the king named is actually Takelot *I*). The king's wife, Karomat D, was a daughter of the former High Priest, Nimlot C; with her, and others, he had at least seven children, four sons and three daughters. Of them, the eldest son, Osorkon B was appointed to the High Priesthood of Amun, while at least two of the daughters married various local dignitaries. The northern part of what had since the Twenty-first Dynasty been part of the Theban polity was in the hands of Ptah-udjankhef, another son of Nimlot C, based at Herakleopolis.

The formal establishment of a Theban monarchy seems to have led to the unleashing of forces that had remained suppressed since the 'troubles' that had followed the death of Masaharta, two centuries before (see p. 156, above). In Takelot II's eleventh regnal year, the High Priest, Prince Osorkon B, was forced to sail southwards from El-Hiba towards Thebes to face some potential 'enemy who will take hold of the office of the High Priest of Amun'. Various opponents had to be suppressed between Ashmunein and Amun's city, where Osorkon offered to his god, and executed various individuals who had been denounced to him by members of his clergy. The bodies of these rebels were burnt, the most horrific posthumous fate that an Egyptian could imagine, depriving, as it did, the dead of their immortality.

Two years later, Osorkon was apparently able to carry out his duties during the three great annual Theban festivals, but at almost the same moment there appeared on the Theban scene a King Pedubast I as a direct rival to Takelot II. Not unsurprisingly, the result was civil war. Hostilities seem to have begun in earnest in Takelot's year 15, with Osorkon in the thick of the fighting, which lasted until year 24, when some kind of agreement allowed the prince to resume his place as High Priest – for a while, at least. That some kind of accommodation had been arrived at is suggested by the fact that Osorkon did not claim the throne on his father's death soon afterwards; instead, one Iuput (I) became formal co-regent with Pedubast I.

The regime of Kings Pedubast and Iuput recognized that of Shoshenq III in the north, mentioning his regnal years (but not his

Fig. 59. Osorkon III, depicted in the act of launching a sacred bark; from Karnak.

name) alongside those of Pedubast. During the period of the war, the *de facto* High Priesthood was held by Harsiese B, probably the grandson of the priest-king of the same name, ignoring the *de joure* rights of Osorkon B. Other offices were given to Pedubast's own son, Pediamenet. The length of time Iuput, whose name recalls that of an earlier high priest, Shoshenq I's son, held kingly titles is unknown, but was probably short. Most probably he lost his position, if not his life, in the renewal of hostilities that occurred only a year or two after Takelot II's death.

The immediate result was Osorkon B's expulsion from Thebes once again, this time for nearly a decade. He was replaced by one Takelot E; also active around this time in the service of

171

Pedubast was a son of Shoshenq III, Pashedbast, who served as his army-chief.

It was not until year 39 of Shoshenq III (c. 800 BC) that Osorkon was able to find the wherewithal to finally regain his inheritance. At some point prior to this, his younger brother, Bakenptah, had managed to secure the governorship of Herakleopolis, dislodging adherents of Pedubast I in the process. Following on from this success, an offensive against Thebes was possible; soon afterwards, to quote a text from Karnak:

> [Osorkon] was within Thebes, celebrating the festival of Amun, in one accord with his brother, the General and Army-leader, Bakenptah .... Then they overthrew everyone who had fought against them.

At long last, Osorkon was in undisputed control of the Thebaid, after some three decades of conflict. Within a short time of his return, the prince-priest had put the seal on his victory by being proclaimed king at Thebes, as Osorkon III.

By now around fifty years old, the king had a number of children, the eldest son being Takelot G, who was immediately installed in his father's former pontificate, serving as High Priest of Amun for the whole of Osorkon III's reign. He was also placed in charge of Herakleopolis, thus giving him undisputed operational control of the Theban realm. Takelot's sister, Shepenwepet (I), later took her place in Amun's clergy, becoming God's Wife. By appointing two of his offspring to head the Theban cult, the king was clearly aiming to ensure that the troubles that had blighted his own priestly career would not return. It seems that the power of the God's Wife was increased at the expense of the High Priest, later ladies appearing to be far more important than their male colleagues, some of whose very identities are uncertain.

Shepenwepet was the daughter of Queen Karoatjet, while Takelot and another brother, Rudamun, were born of a lady named Tentsai. A further child may have been Nimlot (D), a man who was to later obtain the title of 'king' of Ashmunein, in Middle Egypt.

After a quarter-century as king, and now in his mid-seventies, Osorkon appointed the High Priest Takelot co-regent. King Takelot III is to be seen with his father and sister on the walls of the

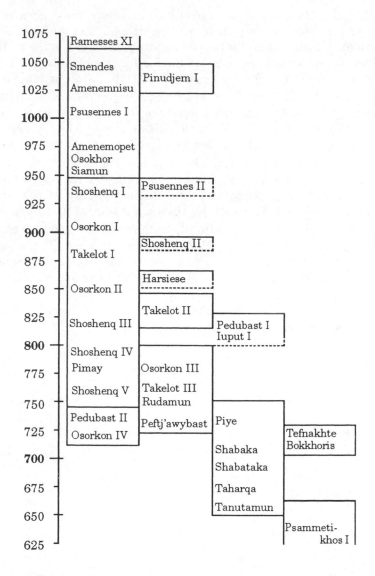

Fig. 60. The overlap of the dynasties of the Third Intermediate Period.

temple of Osiris that they built together at Karnak. As High Priest, the new king was replaced by his own son, Osorkon F,

173

probably the eldest of a large brood of children, most of whom, however, had been born late in his life. Takelot's place at Herakleopolis was taken by Peftjauawybast, clearly a scion of the royal house, who would later be its final ruling representative.

Osorkon III finally died around 769 BC, after a long and adventurous life that well illustrates the breakdown of authority that characterised his era. From later references, he seems to have been buried somewhere in Western Thebes, most probably around Medinet Habu, where Shepenwepet I and later God's Wives were to find rest, as had that earlier Theban king, Harsiese.

After Osorkon's demise, his line continued in the persons of his sons Takelot and Rudamun, the shadowy figure of Iny, and then Peftjauawybast, although by then to all intents and purposes deprived of their Theban heartland. In the far north, the Twenty-second Dynasty was maintained by Shoshenq III's son Pimay, and then a fifth Shoshenq, before giving way to the extremely obscure Twenty-third. By this time, the old family's power over the north was little more than nominal: soon it, and its Theban counterpart were to face an opponent from a wholly unexpected direction whose actions would bring both effectively to an end.

XVI   The Other Egypt

Piye

c.752-717 BC

As we have previously seen, control of Nubia, stretching from Aswan to deep in the modern Sudan, had been a key Egyptian foreign policy objective since Archaic times. During the first two Intermediate Periods it had slipped from the pharaonic grasp, but had soon been brought back under Egyptian control by the first rulers of the Middle and New Kingdoms. By the New Kingdom, Nubia was split into two parts, the northern called Wawat, the southern Kush. The latter name was, however, frequently used to refer to the whole of Nubia, the Viceroy of Kush holding sway over the entire territory.

At the end of the Twentieth Dynasty, the difficulties concerning the Viceroy, Panehsy, had resulted in a number of years' fighting between the forces of the High Priests of Amun and those loyal to the former viceroy. While members of the High Priestly family claimed the viceregal title during the Twenty-first Dynasty, it is unclear how far south their power actually extended, with the likelihood that part of Lower (northern) and all of Upper (southern) Nubia was under the rule of elements related to Panehsy's former regime.

It would appear that some of these assumed the title of (local) pharaoh; the prenomina of the Nubian kings, [...]atiaq and Iry, Menmaetre-setpenamun and Usermaetre-setpenre, are of precisely the same form as those of the recently-ended Ramesside Period (the Nineteenth and Twentieth Dynasties). Likewise, their reliefs recall New Kingdom style, as does one of Queen Karimala, found in the Eighteenth Dynasty temple at Semna. That this formative period was *not* peaceful is indicated by the references to military action in the queen's inscription in the same sanctuary.

These individuals would seem to have flourished around the time of the Twenty-first/early Twenty-second Dynasty in Egypt. They may have belonged to the line of rulers who had begun a series of high-status tumuli at El-Kurru around the end of the Ramesside Period. El-Kurru lies deep in the south of Nubia, and is close to Napata, the capital of Kush since the New Kingdom. The tumulus had been the traditional form of royal tomb in the period of Kushite independence during the Second Intermediate Period, but was replaced some generations on into the new line by what seem to have been mastabas, which continue down to the appearance of a king named Alara in the second quarter of the eighth century BC. Until recently, these mastabas were believed to be the tombs of later queens, but the evidence now seems to point in the direction of their being kingly tombs of the tenth to eighth centuries.

Nothing is known of Alara, but his successor Kashta is a more rounded personality, and the immediate ancestor of what was to become the Twenty-fifth Dynasty. He assumed full pharaonic titles, and rapidly expanded his power into Lower Nubia. His position was soon such that he could have a stela erected in the Elephantine temple of Khnum. His burial place was the last of the royal mastabas to be built at El-Kurru; his successors were to adopt a somewhat different type of tomb.

Kashta was succeeded by Piye, whose name was formerly, and probably wrongly, read as 'Piankhy'. Since the days of Egyptian occupation, the state religion of Kush had been that of Amun-Re, the great god of Thebes, who owned a monumental temple at Napata. In addition to this, the rulers of Kush, although clearly of southern, or at least mainly-southern, race, had adopted the insignia and mores of the pharaonic monarchy of Egypt. Accordingly, it is clear that there was very much a feeling among them that Egypt, and in particular Thebes, was their spiritual home.

At the time Piye ascended his Napatan throne, Egypt was politically in a sorry state. As related in the previous chapter, central control had come to an end, with at least four individuals using the titles of Pharaoh, and a number of local chiefdoms and principalities existing around the country, particularly in the Delta. Confronted with this degradation of what he viewed as his 'mother country', Piye decided to set matters to rights.

Early in his reign, Kushite influence was extended further north to Thebes itself. There, Piye had his sister, Amenirdis I, adopted by the incumbent God's Wife of Amun, Shepenwepet I, as her intended successor, presumably with the acquiescence of the latter lady's brother – King Rudamun of the Theban Twenty-third Dynasty. That both the latter and Piye were recognized at Thebes is demonstrated by the appearance of both their respective regnal years in a graffito referring to their priestly sisters. Piye's position as an effective overlord of southern Egypt may have been recognized as far north as Ashmunein, where the local 'King', Nimlot, owed him some allegiance. After Rudamun's death, the Theban royal line seems to have effectively abandoned their city as a place of permanent residence, the last king of the dynasty, Peftjauawy-bast, making Herakleopolis his seat, apparently as an ally of the Kushite monarch.

A pretext for intervening further north was provided by the southward expansion of Tefnakhte, the Prince of the West, based on the ancient Delta city of Sais. Nominally a subject of Shosh-enq V and his successors at Tanis, in Piye's twentieth regnal year Tefnakhte took control of Memphis, and the old Middle Kingdom centre of Itj-tawy (Lisht), and seems to have seduced to his side Piye's former ally, Nimlot. Since this could be seen as threatening the Kushite king's interests, an army was sent to check Tefnakhte's southward push, something that was achieved by a pair of naval battles in Middle Egypt. Nevertheless, the Saite was left in control of the north, and Nimlot in his city which was, however, rapidly surrounded by Kushite soldiery.

Piye now decided to head downstream to lead the war personally, to displace the troublesome Tefnakhte, and undertake the setting-to-rights of Egypt. After spending New Year at home in Napata, he proceeded to Thebes in time for the great Opet Festival, the high point of the city's religious year, and of great importance to the Amun-devotee, Piye. The arrival of their king in Egypt spurred on the troops further north, who succeeded in capturing at least three towns, killing a son of Tefnakhte in the process.

After leaving Thebes, Piye's first objective was the besieged Ashmunein, and the turncoat Nimlot. Having harangued his army for their lack of success so far, the king then undertook the personal supervision of operations, including the erection of a wooden siege-tower, from which the Kushite archers could fire down into the city. Thus tormented, running short of supplies after what was by now some five months of investiture and, to quote the Kushite account of the campaign, 'foul of nose, without fragrance', Ashmunein surrendered, Nimlot's wife prominent amongst those pleading for mercy.

Nimlot himself then fell to the ground at Piye's feet, bringing with him treasure, a sistrum and a horse as gifts. The latter seems to have been an inspired choice, for Piye was a great horse enthusiast, as is borne out by his reaction when, after his triumphant entry into Ashmunein, he visited Nimlot's stables and found that the horses had been allowed to suffer during the siege:

> I swear ... that it is more grievous in my heart that my horses have suffered hunger than anything that you (Nimlot) have done, in the carrying out of your plans.

This love of horses is found with a number of other Kushite kings, some of whom had their horses buried near their tombs.

Further north, Piye's loyal ally, King Peftjauawybast, had been threatened by the Tefnakhte-Nimlot axis, but his city of Herakleopolis was now relieved, the ruler giving fulsome thanks to the Kushite. The latter was now able, with very little actual fighting, to take the surrender of all the important centres south of Memphis, capturing another son of Tefnakhte at Pisekhem-kheperre, near the entrance to the Fayoum.

All that now lay between Piye and control of the whole Nile valley was the ancient capital, Memphis. The king's demands from afar that the city surrender were met by an attack on the Kushite expeditionary force, and a closure of the gates. Soon afterwards, Tefnakhte gained access under the cover of darkness, installed a garrison of eight thousand men, and departed on horseback – unusually, for the Egyptians generally preferred to use a chariot –

Fig. 61. Nimlot leads a horse as he and his fellow 'kings' submit to Piye. In the lower register kneel Osorkon IV, Iuput II and Peftjauawybast.

bound for the Delta to raise reinforcements.

When Piye arrived the next morning, he was faced by the great walled city, with the water of the river close up to its walls. Long debates ensued as how to best conduct the apparently-inevitable siege, before a way round the problem was noticed. Rapidly, all the masted boats and ships in the Memphite harbour were captured and brought up against the city walls, their rigging being used to scale the fortifications: by the next morning, the whole of Memphis was in Kushite hands. In keeping with his views on the holy nature of his task, one of Piye's first thoughts was to send troops to protect the temple of Ptah, and then to go there himself to be anointed and to worship.

With the capture of the old national capital, most of the local rulers of the Delta came to yield to the Kushite king. The first to arrive were Akunosh of Sebannytos, Pediese of Athribis and Heliopolis and King Iuput II of Leontopolis. Soon afterwards, while Piye was at the sanctuary of the sun-god Re at Heliopolis, there arrived King Osorkon IV, the last representative of the great line

179

begun by Shoshenq I, now reduced to being but one amongst many petty rulers submitting to the representative of a country that had been for generations regarded as barbarian.

Having moved on to Athribis, at the very apex of the Delta, Piye assembled before him the fifteen local rulers who had thus far come to formally submit to him. They were dismissed to go back to their cities to prepare tribute for their new overlord, comprising treasure, exotic produce – and horses! Some of these animals were to be represented in the triumphal reliefs that Piye was later to inscribe on the walls of the temples of Napata.

Now, from amongst these Delta rulers, there was one notable absentee: Tefnakhte. No sooner had his erstwhile allies given themselves up to the southern conqueror than the Saite sent troops into a strategic town in the southern part of his West Delta realm. However, the move was swiftly crushed by Piye, making even Tefnakhte realize that further resistance was useless. Nevertheless, his submission was brought by a messenger: not for him was his fellows' abject prostration before the Kushite king. Furthermore, the oath of allegiance that Tefnakhte had to swear was administered by officials who had to go all the way to Sais; thus, even in defeat, Tefnakhte could maintain his dignity.

A final ceremony of submission was held, at which any remaining centres proclaimed their adhesion to Piye's overlordship. The four individuals who held pharaonic titles also arrived, but only Nimlot was allowed into the royal presence: Osorkon IV (Twenty-third Dynasty), Peftjauawybast (Theban Twenty-third Dynasty/Herakleopolis) and Iuput II (Leontopolis) were dismissed as ritually impure, having eaten fish. Having imposed this final humiliation upon the 'kings' of the ancient line: Piye went home.

Loading his ships with the tribute of Egypt, he sailed southwards, doubtless stopping en-route to receive the homage of his new subjects, finally arriving in Napata, where he set up the great stela that tells us of his exploits. Other works included a second stela, and the series of now-destroyed reliefs in the courtyard of the temple of Amun there, which he took the first steps towards enlarging into the giant temple whose ruin survives today. Apparently satisfied with his work, and his status as ackn-

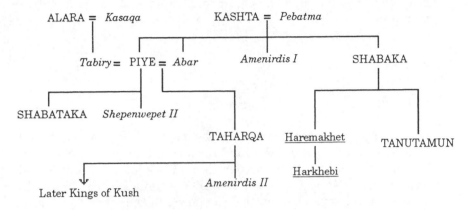

Fig. 62. Genealogical table for the Twenty-fifth Dynasty.

owledged overlord of Egypt, he never again went north, leaving the rule of the country to his vassals.

Some of them certainly remained loyal, in particular at Thebes, where his sister would within a few years become the sole God's Wife, and Herakleopolis, where Peftjauawybast had remained faithful throughout the war with Tefnakhte. It was Tefnakhte who was the problem: within a short time, Piye's old enemy had proclaimed himself king, controlling at least the western Delta and thus founding the Twenty-fourth Dynasty. On his death, eight years later, he was succeeded by his son, Bokkhoris.

It is unknown how Piye reacted to these manoeuvres; perhaps he was content that his holy city of Amun, Thebes, remained loyal to him. At his death, he was buried at El-Kurru, under the first of a long series of royal pyramids that were to be built in the Sudan. Although possibly inspired by Piye having seen the great monuments of Giza and Dahshur, the pyramid more closely resembled the tall, narrow structures that had been built above many private tombs of the New Kingdom. Today, the superstructure of Piye's sepulchre is gone, and his burial chamber open to the sky. No certain remains of his body were discovered when it was excavated by an American expedition in 1917, although his set of dummy canopic jars survived, and evidence to show that the body had been laid upon a bed, in conformity with ancient Nubian tradition.

Taharqa

c. 690-664 BC

Piye's apparent indifference to the rise of the Twenty-fourth Dynasty was not shared by his brother and successor, Shabaka. Within two years of his accession he had headed northwards and, according to Manetho, burnt Bokkhoris to death. Shabaka also seems to have severely curtailed the power of the other 'royal' lines that Piye had left in place: certainly he took up residence in Memphis as the fully-fledged ruler of the united kingdom of Egypt and Kush, symbolised by his adoption of the twin uraeus on his crown.

He was followed on the throne by his nephew, Shabataka, a son of Piye: the Kushites did not follow the Egyptian practice of primogeniture, but passed the throne to a king's brothers before reverting to his son. Since the campaigns of Shoshenq I, Egypt had apparently kept herself largely apart from the politics of Syria-Palestine, increasingly overshadowed by Assyria, to the east. Now, Assyria, under Sennacherib (704-681 BC) was flexing its muscles amongst its rebellious vassals in the Levant, and the new pharaoh decided that the time had come to intervene.

Amongst those who were part of the Egypto-Nubian army that marched into Palestine was the king's younger brother, Taharqa, who had journeyed up from Napata, together with his other siblings, at Shabataka's behest. He was accordingly at 701 BC's Battle of Eltekeh (south-east of Joppa), where Pharaoh's armies, together with those of its local allies, were beaten by the crack Assyrian forces. Any thoughts of a counter-attack while the Assyrians were engaged in reducing Jerusalem were foiled by the return of Sennacherib's forces to guard against just such an eventuality. Taharqa and the army thus retired to Egypt, to avoid further conflict with Assyria for another two decades.

Following his brother's death, Taharqa became king, being

Fig. 63. King Taharqa, on a chapel from the king's temple at Kawa.

crowned at Memphis in 690 BC, at around the age of thirty. Six years later, it is recorded that rain fell in Nubia, something that has always been unusual; extreme wetness even further south, around the source of the Nile in the depths of Africa led to the same year seeing a particularly high inundation. While a good flood was desirable, one that exceeded a certain height was not, given the danger of dykes and other protective barriers being overwhelmed, with the consequent flooding of habitations. In this case, however, the god Amun was credited with ameliorating the effects, granting freedom from pests and giving a bumper harvest. The same year also saw a visit to Egypt by Taharqa's mother, Abar, whom the king had not seen since leaving Napata at Shabataka's command, eighteen years before.

At Thebes, the tradition of installing one of the reigning king's

183

close female relations as the heir-apparent to the current God's Wife of Amun was continued, Taharqa's daughter, Amenirdis (II), being adopted by her aunt, Shepenwepet II. Male Priesthoods of Amun also remained in the royal family: Shabaka had made his son, Haremakhet, High Priest, and he was followed by his own offspring, Harkhebi. As the latter's immediate subordinate, Taharqa appointed Prince Nesishutefnut, one of his own sons, as Second Prophet.

Taharqa built extensively, throughout his dual kingdom. The temples of Napata were greatly enlarged, with new sanctuaries established in a number of Nubian towns, including Qasr Ibrim. At Kawa, the New Kingdom temples were extensively renovated, the project having been in the king's mind since initially visiting them during his first voyage north. In Egypt itself, major additions were made to the temples of Amun-Re and Montju at Karnak, at Medinet Habu, and Memphis.

The artistic work of Taharqa and his fellow Kushites displays many archaistic features, providing the prototype for the even more extensive use of the past as an inspiration that is found in the next, Twenty-sixth, Dynasty. Indeed, certain blocks imitate Old Kingdom work so well that there has been some debate as to which century – the eighth or twenty-sixth – they really belong. There were also other kinds of antiquarian investigation, including the compilation of the so-called 'Memphite Theology' under Shabaka, allegedly copied from a worm-eaten papyrus of Old Kingdom date. Also clearly derived from the past was the Kushite kings' continued use of the pyramid-tomb, their monuments increasing in size and elaboration as the dynasty progressed. Indeed, the royal line would continue to employ this form of sepulchre long after they ceased to rule Egypt: the last of all true pyramids was built at Meroë in the Sudan around AD 350, three thousand years after the first such structure had been built for King Djoser at Saqqara.

In spite of being seemingly firmly established on their northern throne, the nemesis of the Kushite kings was approaching in the shape of the Assyrian king, Esarhaddon (680-669 BC). Early in his reign, Esarhaddon had begun a programme of eliminating rebellious vassals in Syria-Palestine, and he clearly regarded Egypt as a source of trouble. Thus, in 674 he attempted to invade Taharqa's kingdom, but was successfully repulsed. The Kushite king took a close interest in his army, quite probably with a view to the Assyrian threat which he had seen at first hand at the Battle of Eltekeh, as is shown by a stela which describes his reviewing and exercising with his troops in the Western Desert.

Four years later, the Assyrian king made a further strike against Egypt; this time he reached Memphis, forcing Taharqa to retreat upstream, and capturing one of his sons, and a brother. The Delta still contained the representatives of the various dynasties who had been humbled by Piye and Shabaka, and these were seconded by Esarhaddon as his local rulers. However, as soon as the Assyrian had returned to Iraq, Taharqa reimposed himself on the north, being particularly fortunate in that Esarhaddon died before being able to reach Egypt to oppose him.

Regrettably, the new Assyrian monarch, Assurbanipal, was not prepared to forget about Egypt, and launched a fresh campaign in 665/666. Defeated in battle, Taharqa was forced to retreat once

Fig. 64. The pyramid of Taharqa at Nuri.

185

more, this time to Thebes, whence Assurbanipal followed him. Unable to stand against the invader, Taharqa had no choice but to fall back on his ancestral realm and return to Napata. The Egyptian rulers were thus forced to once again acknowledge Assurbanipal as their overlord, although some, particularly Nekho I of Sais, seem to have preferred the Assyrian to the Kushite in this role. In Nekho's case this is probably not surprising, since he seems to have been a direct descendant of the bane of the Kushites' Egyptian ambitions, Tefnakhte.

Those who did not take Nekho's line took advantage of Assurbanipal's departure to begin plotting Taharqa's restoration, thereby provoking the local Assyrian representatives to arrest the Delta princes wholesale. Some were put to death in Egypt, and the rest sent to the Assyrian capital, Nineveh, for execution. Only Nekho I and his son, Psametjik, were judged as having remained loyal, and rewarded with the rule of the western Delta, along with Memphis.

Nevertheless, Taharqa seems by now to have been able to reclaim the rule of Thebes, but his days were numbered: the king died in 664 BC and was succeeded by his nephew, Tanutamun. Taharqa was not buried alongside his ancestors at El-Kurru. Instead, he established a new royal necropolis a few kilometres up-river, at Nuri. There he erected the largest of all the Kushite pyramids: at 52 metres square, however, it was still considerably smaller than any of the kingly pyramids in Egypt. It was equipped with a particularly elaborate substructure, incorporating a columned burial hall, from which were recovered many elements of the king's funerary equipment, including a few fragments of his skull, the inlay of his coffins, his canopic jars and hundreds of shabti figures.

XVII   The Dimming Glory

Psammetikhos I

664-610 BC

On the death of his uncle, the new king, Tanutamun, immediately sailed from Napata to reimpose Kushite rule over the whole of Egypt. Having secured the southern cities, he took Memphis and then pressed on into the Delta. As the key Assyrian vassal, Nekho I was rapidly put to death, and his son, Psametjik, forced to escape to Nineveh, the remaining local princes accepting the Kushite as their ruler.

However, Assurbanipal was not slow in sending an army to once more subdue Egypt, succeeding in driving Tanutamun back down to Thebes, and then into Nubia. In doing so, they undertook to sack Amun's city, carrying masses of loot back to Iraq, and providing the Old Testament prophets with an enduring template for the wreck of a former imperial city.

Amongst those who entered Egypt with Assurbanipal's army was Nekho's son, since his father's execution, King Psammetikhos I, regarded by posterity as the founder of the Twenty-sixth Dynasty. As such he took over the rule of Sais and Memphis, the rest of Egypt being under the sway of the descendants of the men who had submitted to Piye, nearly a century before.

Psammetikhos I was to all appearances a loyal subject of Assurbanipal, even possessing an alternate Assyrian name, Nabu-shezibanni. However, it is quite clear that, like his ancestor, Tefnakhte, he had a wider agenda than being a vassal, and the first decade of the reign saw the gradual extension of Saite rule throughout Egypt. In this he was helped by the fact that, beset by the threat of a resurgent Babylon to their south, Assyria was no longer able to assert herself concerning Egyptian internal affairs:

within fifty years, Assyria would be no more. By his ninth regnal year, Psammetikhos I could claim to be the true pharaoh of a united, independent, Egypt.

Herodotus records that Psammetikhos' assumption of sole rule was in fulfilment of an oracle that stated that the first of the 'twelve' kinglets who had previously ruled Egypt to pour a libation from a bronze vessel in the temple of Hephaestus (= Ptah, at Memphis) would become master of all Egypt:

> It was the last day of the festival, and when the moment for pouring the libation had come, the High Priest, in going to fetch the golden cups that were always used for the purpose, made a mistake and brought one too few, so that Psammetikhos, who was standing last in the row, did not get one. As was their custom, all the kings were wearing bronze helmets, and Psammetikhos, finding himself without a cup, quite innocently took off his helmet, held it out to receive the wine and made his libation.

The Greek writer goes on to tell that the military power which aided Psammetikhos's assumption of full authority took the form of Hellenic mercenaries: certainly the Twenty-sixth, or Saite, Dynasty was always particularly friendly with the peoples of the Aegean.

The adhesion of Thebes, the first and last stronghold of Kushite influence in Egypt, was marked in year 9 by the adoption of Psammetikhos I's daughter, Nitokris, as the ultimate successor of the current God's Wife of Amun, Shepenwepet II, and her heir Amenirdis II. Together with the High Priest, Harkhebi, grandson of Shabaka, they were the last scions of the Twenty-fifth Dynasty still holding power in Egypt, and who had thus far continued to use the regnal years of the now long-departed Tanutamun for dating purposes. However, the Thebaid had been effectively an independent polity since the Kushite's flight, with the leading role taken by the Fourth Prophet of Amun, Montjuemhat. In the events that culminated in this formal southern recognition of his rule, Psammetikhos I was aided by his allies, the 'shipmasters' of Herakleopolis, Pediese and his son, Somtutefnakhte. Through them, his control of Middle Egypt was assured.

The remaining four decades of the reign were concerned with the consolidation of power, within a country that had not seen true

Fig. 65. Head of a king of the Late Period.

central control for very many years. Building-work was carried o u t on a scale only possible in the context of a unified state, many sites revealing elements of Psammetikhos I's constructions. In particular, we have the Delta forts of Naukratis and Daphnae, and a southern counterpart at Elephantine. On the religious front, the king was responsible for a major extension of the Serapeum of Saqqara, the burial-place of the Apis bulls.

Foreign affairs were essentially concerned with maintaining the country's independence, hence an expedition into Lower Nubia, perhaps to discourage any thoughts the Kushite king might have had of staging a come-back in the north. In the north-east, the troubles of Assyria became such that Egypt became her ally in an attempt to hold back the power of Babylon. Through this, Egypt obtained control of the Palestinian coast, and fought on the side of her former conqueror in the last years of Psammetikhos I's reign. Action was also required on the Libyan frontier against the threat of fugitive Delta princes; indeed, at various potentially sensitive points, garrisons were installed to guarantee security, tying in with the fort-building already mentioned.

The Saite regime continued the archaistic tendencies of the previous dynasty. In the formulation of their names, the simple approach of the Old Kingdom was preferred to the elaboration of the New Kingdom and earlier Third Intermediate Period: contrast the titularies of Osorkon II and Psammetikhos I –

OSORKON II:	*Horus*	Ka-nakht-merymaet-sekha-su-re-em-nesu-er-seped-tawi
	Nebty	Sema-pesesheti-mi-sieset-demedjef-sekhemty-em-hetep
	Bik-nub	Werpehty-huy-Montju
	Prenomen	(Usermaetre-meryamun)∤
	Nomen	(Osorkon-sibast-meryamun)∤
PSAMMETIKHOS I:	*Horus*	Aib
	Nebty	Neba
	Bik-nub	Qenu
	Prenomen	(Wahibre)∤
	Nomen	(Psametjik)∤

This regard for the past was extended in other directions as well, with sculpture executed in styles recalling earlier eras, and in some cases direct copies being made of ancient works. The pyramids were investigated, a new entrance passage being quarried under the Step Pyramid, and a new coffin provided for the plundered mummy of Mykerinos.

Psammetikhos I had married Mehtemweskhet, daughter of Harsiese S, High Priest at Heliopolis, and on his death in 610, he was succeeded by his son, Nekho II. At fifty-four years, his had been one of the longest reigns in Egyptian history, and one of the most important for its reunification of the country after some four centuries of greater or lesser fragmentation. He was laid to rest within the precincts of the temple of Neith at Sais, but of his burial, only one or two shabti-figures are known.

Amasis

570-526 BC

Nekho II followed his father's policy of intervening in Syria-Palestine in aid of the Assyrians, and doubtless his own sphere of influence. However, although at one point he managed to push as far north as the Euphrates, he was later pushed back, and left with his border at Gaza. His short-lived successor, Psammetikhos II, is best known for a campaign into Nubia against the still-powerful Kushites; he was additionally responsible for the desecration of many of the standing monuments of the Twenty-fifth Dynasty. In Syria-Palestine, he undertook an expedition which seems to have been intended to mark Egypt's continued concern for the region in the face of the continued Babylonian threat.

He was followed by his son, Apries, who also took an interest in the north-east, and undertook campaigns by land and sea against the Levantine coast. He was also, however, concerned with Libya, and mounted a campaign which was to end in disaster for the king. The expedition itself had been a military failure, which was blamed on the king himself; a revolt ensued, and the General

Amasis (Ahmose), who had been sent to put it down, found himself proclaimed pharaoh.

Having mutilated the nobleman who had brought the news of Amasis' acceptance of his soldiers' acclamation, King Apries advanced from his residence to meet the usurper, at the head of an army of Aegean mercenaries. The two protagonists' forces met in January/February 570 BC somewhere in the north-west Delta, those of Apries being forced to retreat. On the basis of this victory, Amasis occupied the capital, Sais, and began his formal reign, although initially recognized only as far south as El-Hiba.

Apries was, however, still held to be king by those in the south of Egypt, and may have remained ensconced in his massive palace-complex at Memphis. It was perhaps from there that he launched his October 570 attempt to regain his throne, again aided by Greek troops. However, Amasis was once more the victor, Apries this time escaping abroad, eventually turning up at the court of Nebuchadnezzar of Babylon.

With the rival monarch having fled his kingdom, Amasis was now able to claim the loyalty of the whole of Egypt, Thebes switching allegiance between 19 October and 9 December of 570. However, the wretched Apries was still not finished, for in March 567 he advanced on Egypt in the company of a Babylonian army. To counter this, Amasis raised his forces and, for the final time, defeated his rival. It would appear that Apries was captured and initially allowed to live. However, according to Herodotus:

> The Egyptians complained that he did wrong by maintaining a man who was the greatest enemy both to them and [Amasis]; therefore he delivered Apries to the people, who strangled him.

Nevertheless, Amasis buried him with kingly honours in the royal necropolis at Sais, like the tombs of the kings of Tanis in the courtyard of the principal temple, at Sais dedicated to the goddess Neith.

Now free of any rival, Amasis was free to complete the consolidation of his throne as the very last great pharaoh. Since the time of the founder of the dynasty, Greeks had played a prominent part, not least as mercenaries in the army, and most recently on the side of the late King Apries in the civil war. They

Fig. 66. Amasis, as depicted on the façade of the chapel of Osiris-Wennefer-nebdjefa at Karnak.

had also become heavily involved in Egypt's commerce, with Aegean settlement encouraged by Psammetikhos I in the area of Naukratis. Amasis took this a step further by concentrating all Greek trade on that city, which thus took upon itself a largely Hellenic appearance. Apart from anything else, the establishment of such a centre made the derivation of royal revenues from the Greeks' trading activities simple – and lucrative.

Amasis was particularly active in cultivating the states of the Aegean, and exchanged gifts with many of them, additionally bringing Cyprus into the Egyptian orbit. This northern dimension to the king's policy doubtless had much to do with maintaining allies against the threat from the east, posed by Babylon and the rapidly expanding Persians.

At home, Amasis was a builder of some note, contributing to the splendours of Memphis, Abydos, Koptos, Karnak, and a number of Delta sites, amongst others. Like his predecessors, he built his tomb at Sais; although no trace of it has ever been found, we have Herodotus's description:

> [It is] a great cloistered building of stone, decorated with pillars carved in the imitation of palm-trees, and other costly ornaments. Within the cloister is a chamber with double doors, and behind the doors stands the sepulchre.

Amasis was the son of the Lady Takheredeneset, and married two women, Tentheta and Nakhtsebastetru. By them, he had a number of children, his prospective successor, Psametjik, the General Ahmose, and Pasenkhonsu. Ahmose and his mother, Nakhtsebastetru, were buried in tomb LG 83 at Giza, their sarcophagi now being in St Petersburg. A possible further wife, perhaps a daughter of Apries, was Khedebneithireretbeneret, buried at Saqqara. A daughter was Nitokris II, who may have gone to Thebes for adoption as prospective God's Wife by the incumbent, Ankhesenneferibre, sister of Apries.

Amasis' last years were clouded by the steady advance of the Persians, who had now long-since disposed of Babylon, conquered the Greek states of Asia and were now the sole great power of that continent. Led by Kambyses, they marched on Egypt, reaching the frontier almost at the moment of Amasis' death, after a reign of forty-four years.

194

The reign of the new king, Psammetikhos III, was short; he attempted to resist the invasion, but was forced to surrender at Memphis. Taken prisoner, he was at first allowed to live on at the Persian court; however, found to be plotting to restore his throne, he was put to death.

Herodotus reports that on occupying Sais, Kambyses had the mummy of Amasis exhumed and:

> subjected to every indignity, such as lashing with whips and the plucking of its hairs, until the executioners were weary. At last, as the corpse had been embalmed and would not fall to pieces under the blows, Kambyses ordered it to be burnt.

This is not unlike the fate that one fancies may have been meted out to the body of the disgraced Akhenaten, eight centuries before, not to mention Osorkon B's opponents (see pp. 107-9, 172, above); however, there must remain some doubt as to the truth of the story, in spite of the clear evidence of the erasure of the names of Amasis from numerous inscriptions. This doubt arises from another atrocity attributed to Kambyses, the wounding and subsequent death of the sacred Apis bull of Memphis. While it is clear that an Apis *did* die under Kambyses, the stela from its burial is dated to the reign of him as a proper pharaoh, which fits in badly with Herodotus' tale that the burial was carried out by the priests in secret.

Additionally, a contemporary inscription, that of Udjahorresneith, seems to indicate that the Persian king, regarded as the founder of the Twenty-seventh Dynasty, respected the Egyptians' religious sensibilities. Regrettably, the whole business is so distorted by the propaganda of each side that it is difficult to get at the truth.

XVIII Native Sunset

Nektanebo I

380-363 BC

The Persian kings retained control of Egypt for something over a century. Initially, particularly under Darios I, things seem to have run fairly smoothly; the Persian king played the part of pharaoh sufficiently well to maintain a degree of loyalty from his Egyptian subjects. This was not, however, the case with his successor, Xerxes I, who was remembered as an 'enemy' for confiscating certain important temple-estates.

Accordingly, the reigns of the following Persian monarchs, Artaxerxes I, Xerxes II and Darios II, were all marked by revolts. The first of these Persian monarchs was faced by one Inaros, who, in the course of his rebellion succeeded in killing the Persian governor, or satrap. Inaros was eventually captured and executed, but was replaced by one Amyrtaios as a focus of native discontent.

Finally, soon after the accession of Artaxerxes II in 405, another Amyrtaios, of Sais, arose and achieved at least nominal independence as the sole king of the Twenty-eighth Dynasty. The tenuous nature of his position is shown by the fact that, three years later, Egyptian soldiers were still serving in the Persian army.

Amyrtaios was not alone in aspiring to the pharaonic throne, for in 399, Nepherites I seems to have captured the Twenty-eighth Dynasty monarch, brought him to Memphis, and there executed him. Thus he began his own, Twenty-ninth, Dynasty. The new line hailed from Mendes, where the tomb of the founder has recently been firmly identified by the University of Toronto expedition.

Nepherites I and his successors, in particular Akhoris, succeeded in maintaining their position in the face of attempts by

Artaxerxes II to regain control over Egypt. Akhoris was sufficiently able to unite the country to embark on a building programme, but his latter years were disturbed by revolts, and in them lay the seed of the end of the dynasty. The General Nakhtnebef, who had suppressed a revolt in Akhoris' eighth regnal year, turned on his royal masters, bringing to an abrupt end the reign of Nepherites II, and becoming king as Nektanebo I.

The new dynastic founder hailed from the town of Sebannytos, and was the son of the Generalissimo Djedhor, perhaps a descendant of Nepherites I. He was doubtless a close associate of the Athenian general, Khabrias, who had commanded the Greek mercenaries that formed the core of Akhoris' army in the latter part of his reign.

The new king's military background stood Nektanebo in good stead when, in 373, Artaxerxes II made an attempt to forcibly return Egypt to the Persian fold, in spite of the pharaoh's loss of his putative father-in-law's skills, when the latter was recalled to advanced into the eastern Delta, but failed to press home their advantage. While the Persians were still consolidating their forces, the onset of Nile inundation was used by the Egyptians to help them push the invaders back, thus securing the frontier for the remainder of Nektanebo I's reign.

Like Psammetikhos I before him, Nektanebo was consciously archaistic in his titulary, using the same prenomen as Sesostris I of the Twelfth Dynasty. He also built extensively, the artistic style used moving away from classic Egyptian proportions towards those more readily associated with monuments of the later Greek domination of Egypt. Amongst his monuments are the earliest surviving parts of the temples of Philae, and a considerable number of sculptures which found their way to the Hellenistic capital of Alexandria, and later to Rome, where they formed the basis of some of the earliest assessments of Ancient Egyptian art.

Towards the end of the reign, an attempt was made to renew old alliances between Egypt and the Hellenic powers of Athens and Sparta, with a view to opposing the next adventure on the part of the Persians, who were certain not to abandon what they regarded to be their rebellious province.

Fig. 67. King Nektanebo I offers to the gods in his entrance to the temple of Isis on the island of Philae. The Greek graffiti and Christian cross mark the passing of the ancient civilization six centuries after the death of the last-but-two native king of Egypt.

198

Nektanebo I was probably buried at Sebannytos, but such debris of his tomb as have survived were dispersed in antiquity. A few shabtis are known, while the broken remains of his sarcophagus have been recovered from reuse in various buildings in Cairo, showing it to be a near-copy of Eighteenth Dynasty examples. This fashion was also adopted by other notables of the period, one Hapymen owning a sarcophagus (now in the British Museum) whose external decoration was clearly copied from the coffer of Tuthmosis III, made over a thousand years previously.

Nektanebo II

360-342 BC

Nektanebo I was succeeded by his son, Teos, who had played a major role in his father's last few years on the throne, latterly as coregent. He went on the offensive against the Persians, supporting revolts against Artaxerxes II, and took to the field at the head of an army containing a large contingent of Greek mercenaries, under King Agesilaos of Sparta. In the pharaoh's absence, Egypt was left in the hands of Teos' brother, Tjahapimu, quite possibly an elder sibling, passed over in favour of a child born after Nektanebo I's accession to the throne. Khabrias had now returned to Egypt, and lent his support to the new king's forces.

To finance his war, Teos had been obliged to levy heavy taxes at home, and these were used by his brother as a pretext for raising the country in revolt. Tjahapimu's son, Nakhthorheb, was serving with the royal army, by now in Syria, and succeeded in winning both his own men, and the Greeks over to the rebel side. Nakhthorheb thus became king as Nektanebo II, the deposed Teos fleeing to the court of his erstwhile enemy, Artaxerxes II of Persia, where he was treated with honour.

Nektanebo II's usurpation was taken by an un-named individual from Mendes as the cue to make his own attempt on the throne, perhaps as a scion of the former Twenty-ninth Dynasty which hailed from that city. A brief civil war included the new king's being besieged in Tanis, although soon succoured by the for-

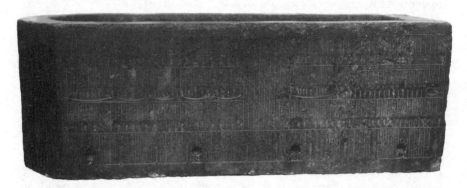

Fig. 68. The sarcophagus of Nektanebo II, never used by its owner and eventually used as a ritual bath.

ces of his friend, the Spartan king. The next threat came from the deposed Teos, acting as a Persian proxy, but after the former pharaoh's death, Nektanebo's Greek forces again managed to maintain Egypt's independence – for the time being.

The king continued Nektanebo I's constructional programme, with monuments throughout Egypt; at some point he buried his probable mother, Udjashu, in a fine sarcophagus, whose remains are now in the Cairo Museum. However, the threat of Persia remained: finally, in the autumn of 343, the Persian king, Artaxerxes III, was successful in penetrating northern Egypt. Nektanebo II was driven out of Memphis and retreated to Upper Egypt, from where he was able to stage a short-lived come-back after Artaxerxes returned home at the end of the campaigning season. The Persians returned however, and Nektanebo II was forced to retreat southwards into Nubia, presumably finding refuge at the Kushite court. As usual, he had begun the preparation of his sarcophagus many years before, and this massive monument was left behind. Its later history is most curious, since by the seventeenth century AD, if not earlier, it had been installed in Alexandria's Attaria Mosque, and was serving as a ritual bath, with holes bored in its lower part to allow the water out. It was taken over by the British in 1800 along with other antiquities, including the famed Rosetta Stone, and came to lie in the British Museum. However, its presence in Alexandria has given rise to various suggestions that it might once have held the body of Alexander the Great. Although without real evidence, the idea that the last Pharaoh's sarcophagus might have ended up sheltering the corpse of the conqueror whose activities closed a whole era of antiquity is not without its attractions!

Epilogue

With the departure of King Nektanebo II, Egypt's independence was over for one and three-quarter millennia. The Persians were to rule for some ten more years before being expelled by Alexander the Great of Macedon. At the break-up of that great conqueror's empire, Egypt fell into the hands of his general, Ptolemy, son of Lagos, who founded a Hellenistic line that was to control Egypt for three centuries. Not a drop of Egyptian blood flowed in the veins of the myriad Ptolemies and Kleopatras who formed the three-hundred-year Ptolemaic Dynasty, and although they may be seen in full pharaonic garb on the many temples they built or restored, it is clear that their regime was in all meaningful ways Hellenic in outlook. On the other hand, Egyptian models continued to be followed in many aspects of administration, and native law remained in use, alongside that brought by the Ptolemies and their Greek settlers.

The latter part of the Ptolemaic Dynasty was marred by endemic fighting within the royal family, whose struggles brought the country within the orbit of Rome. The dalliance of the last of the Ptolemies, Kleopatra VII, with Julius Caesar and Marcus Antonius, made the final act inevitable. In 30 BC, Egypt fell to Octavian, soon to be the Emperor Augustus, and was for the next six centuries part of the Roman and Byzantine Empires. Although now stripped of any vestige of independence, the emperors would continue to be represented as pharaohs on the walls of the temples, worshipping the age-old gods, until the abolition of the ancient religion in the fourth century AD.

Now a formally Christian country, Egypt next fell into Arab hands in 640, the gradually-islamicised state passing in and out of periods of *de facto* self-rule, until becoming a province of the Ottoman Empire in 1517. In the aftermath of the Napoleonic Wars, during which Egypt had been temporarily occupied by the

French, the *Wali* (Governor) Mohammed Ali secured for himself an extremely large measure of freedom from the authority of the Turkish Sultan, his successors being raised to the dignity of *Khedive* (Viceroy). Regrettably, their mismanagement of the country's economy was to place Egypt under the effective control of the British in the latter part of the nineteenth century. In the wake of the Turkish declaration of war on the United Kingdom in 1914, Egypt became a formal British Protectorate, with the *Khedive* promoted to Sultan.

The formal re-institution of an Egyptian monarchy, in the person of King Fuad I (formerly the Sultan Ahmed Fuad), came about in 1922, but true national freedom was not achieved for some decades, until the overt and covert rule of the British had ended. A republic was declared in 1953, following the deposition of King Farouk I, and the brief rule of his infant son, Fuad II: the very last of all those individuals who could claim to have been a 'Monarch of the Nile'.

Chronology and
the Kings of Dynastic Egypt

NOTE: Except for the earliest dynasties, where the Horus name is given, the first name quoted for each king is his *prenomen*; the second is his *nomen*, usually the name bestowed at birth.

		Conjectural Dates	Regnal Years
PALAEOLITHIC PERIOD		500,000-5500	
PREDYNASTIC PERIOD			
Badarian/Merimda/Fayoum A		5500-3800	
Naqada Ia/b		3800-3500	
Naqada Ic, IIa/b		3550-3400	
Naqada IIc		3400-3300	
Naqada IId1/2		3300-3200	
Naqada IIIa1-IIIc2		3200-3050	
ARCHAIC PERIOD			
Dynasty I			
Horus Narmer		3050-	
Horus Aha		:	
Horus Djer	Itit	:	
Horus Djet	Iti	:	
Horus Den	Semti	:	
Horus Anedjib	Merpibia	:	
Horus Semerkhet	Irinetjer	:	
Horus Qaa	Qebh	-2813	
Dynasty II			
Horus Hotepsekhemwy	Baunetjer	2813-	
Horus Nebre	Kakau	:	
Horus Ninetjer	Ninetjer	:	
?	Weneg	:	
?	Sened	:	
Horus Sekhemib/		:	
Seth Peribsen	Peribsen	:	
?	Neferkare	-2709	

?	Neferkasokar	2709-2701	8
?	?	2701-2690	11
Horus and Seth			
Khasekhemwy	Nebwyhetepimyef	2690-2663	27

OLD KINGDOM
Dynasty III

Horus Netjerkhet	Djoser	2662-	
Horus Sanakht	Nebka	:	
Horus Sekhemkhet	Djoser-ti	:	6
Horus Khaba	Teti?	:	6
?		:	
Horus Qahedjet?	Huni	-2597	24

Dynasty IV

Horus Nebmaet	Seneferu	2597-2547	50
Horus Medjedu	Kheops	2547-2524	23
Horus Kheper	Djedefre	2524-2516	8
Horus Userib	Khephren	2516-2493	23
Horus Kakhet	Mykerinos	2493-2475	18
Horus Shepseskhet	Shepseskaf	2475-2471	4

Dynasty V

Horus Irimaet	Userkaf	2471-2464	7
Horus Nebkhau	Sahure	2464-2452	12
Neferirkare	Kakai	2452-2442	10
Shepseskare	Isi	2442-2435	7
Horus Neferkhau	Neferefre	2435-2432	3
Niuserre	Ini	2432-2421	11
Menkauhor	Ikauhor	2421-2413	8
Djedkare	Isesi	2413-2385	28
Horus Wadjtawy	Unas	2385-2355	30

Dynasty VI

Horus Seheteptawy	Teti	2355-2343	12
Nefersahor/Meryre	Pepy I	2343-2297	46
Merenre	Nemtyemsaf I	2297-2290	7
Neferkare	Pepy II	2290-2196	94
Merenre?	Nemtyemsaf II	2196-2195	1

FIRST INTERMEDIATE PERIOD
Dynasty VII/VIII

Netjerkare	?	2195-	
Menkare?	Nitokris	:	

Neferkare	?	:	
Neferkare	Neby	:	
Djedkare	Shemay	:	
Neferkare	Khendu	:	
Merenhor	?	:	
Nikare	?	:	
Neferkare	Tereru	:	
Neferkahor	?	:	
Neferkare	Pepysonbe	:	
Neferkamin	Anu	:	
Qakare	Ibi	:	4
Wadjkare	?	:	
Neferkauhor	Khuihapy	:	
Neferirkare	?	-2160	

Dynasties IX/X

Meryibre	Akhtoy I	2160-	
Neferkare	?	:	
Wahkare	Akhtoy II	:	
?	Senenen ...	:	
Neferkare	Akhtoy III	:	
Mery...	Akhtoy IV	:	
(Various)	(Various)	:	
?	Meryhathor	:	
Nebkaure	Akhtoy V	:	
Merykare	?	:	
?	?	-2040	

Dynasty XIa

Horus Tepya	Montjuhotpe I	2160-	
Horus Sehertawy	Inyotef I	-2123	
Horus Wahankh	Inyotef II	2123-2074	49
Horus Nakhtnebtepnefer	Inyotef III	2074-2066	8

MIDDLE KINGDOM
Dynasty XIb

Nebhepetre	Montjuhotpe II	2066-2014	52
Sankhkare	Montjuhotpe III	2014-2001	13
Nebtawyre	Montjuhotpe IV	2001-1994	7

Dynasty XII

Sehetepibre	Ammenemes I	1994-1964	30
Kheperkare	Sesostris I	1974-1929	45
Nubkhaure	Ammenemes II	1932-1896	36
Khakheperre	Sesostris II	1900-1880	20

Khakaure	Sesostris III	1881-1840	41
Nimaetre	Ammenemes III	1842-1794	48
Maekherure	Ammenemes IV	1798-1785	13
Sobkkare	Sobkneferu	1785-1781	4

Dynasty XIII

Sekhemre-khutawi	Sobkhotpe I	1781-	3
Sekhemkare	Sonbef	:	3
Nerikare	?	:	1
Sekhemkare	Ammenemes V	:	3
Sehetepibre	Qemau	:	2
Sankhibre	Ammenemes VI	:	
Smenkare	Nebnuni	:	
?	Iufeni	:	
Hotepibre	Sihornedjhiryotef	:	
Swadjkare	?	:	
Nedjemibre	?	:	
Khaankhre	Sobkhotpe II	:	
Sekhemre-khutawi	Renisonbe	:	
Auibre	Hor	:	
Sedjefakare	Ammenemes VII	:	
Khutawire	Wegaf	:	
Userkare/Nikhanimaetre	Khendjer	:	
Smenkhkare	Imyromesha	:	
Sehotepkare	Inyotef IV	:	
Meryibre	Seth(y)	:	
Sekhemre-swadjtawi	Sobkhotpe III	:	3
Khasekhemre	Neferhotpe I	:	11
Menwadjre	Sihathor	:	
Khaneferre	Sobkhotpe IV	:	
Merhotepre	Sobkhotpe V	:	
Khahetepre	Sobkhotpe VI	:	4
Wahibre	Iaib	:	10
Merneferre	Aya	:	23
Merhetepre	Ini	:	2
Sankhenre	Sewadjtu		
Mersekhemre	Ined		
Sewadjkare	Hori		
Merkaure	Sobkhotpe VII	:	
Mershepsesre	Ini	:	
Mersekhemre	Neferhotpe II	:	
[5 unknown kings]		:	
Mer[...]re	?	:	
Merkheperre	?	:	

Merkare	?	:
?		:
Sewadjare	Mentuhotpe V	:
[...]mesre	?	:
[...]maetre	Ibi	:
[...]webenre	Hor[..]	:
Se[...]kare	?	:
Seheqaenre	Sankhptahi	:
Sekhaenre	[...]s	:
Sewahenre	Senebmiu	-1650

SECOND INTERMEDIATE PERIOD
Dynasty XV

-	Semqen?	1650-	
-	Sakirhar	:	
Seuserenre	Khyan	:	
Nebkhepeshre/			
Aqenenre/Auserre	Apophis	1585-1545	40
?	Khamudy	1545-1535	

Dynasty XVI

?	?	1650-
Sekhemre-smentawi	Djehuty	:
Sekhemre-sewosertawi	Sobkhotpe VIII	:
Sekhemre-seankhtawi	Neferhotpe III	:
Sankhenre	Montjuhotepi	:
Swadjenre	Nebiriau I	:
Neferkare?	Nebiriau II	:
Semenre	?	:
Seuserenre	Bebiankh	:
Sekhemreshedwaset	?	:
Djedhotepre	Dedumose I	:
Djedneferre	Dedumose II	:
Djedankhre	Montjuemsaf	:
Merankhre	Montjuhotpe VI	:
Seneferibre	Sesostris IV	-1590

Dynasty XVII

Sekhemre-wahkhau	Rehotpe	1585-
Sekhemre-shedtawi	Sobkemsaf I	:
Sekhemre-wepmaet	Inyotef V	:
Nubkheperre	Inyotef VI	:
Sekhemre-heruhirmaet	Inyotef VII	:
Sekhemre-wadjkhau	Sobkemsaf II	:

208

Senakhtenre	Taa I	-1558	
Seqenenre	Taa II	1558-1553	5
Wadjkheperre	Kamose	1553-1549	4

NEW KINGDOM
Dynasty XVIII

Nebpehtire	Amosis	1549-1524	25
Djeserkare	Amenophis I	1524-1503	21
Akheperkare	Tuthmosis I	1503-1491	12
Akheperenre	Tuthmosis II	1491-1479	12
Menkheper(en)re	Tuthmosis III	1479-1424	54
(Maetkare	Hatshepsut	1472-1457)	
Akheperure	Amenophis II	1424-1398	26
Menkheperure	Tuthmosis IV	1398-1388	10
Nebmaetre	Amenophis III	1388-1348	40
Neferkheperure-waenre	Amenophis IV/ Akhenaten	1360-1343	17
(Ankhkheperure	Smenkhkare/ Neferneferuaten	1346-1343	3)
Nebkheperre	Tutankhamun	1343-1333	10
Kheperkheperure	Ay	1333-1328	5
Djeserkheperure-setpenre	Horemheb	1328-1298	30

Dynasty XIX

Menpehtire	Ramesses I	1298-1296	2
Menmaetre	Sethos I	1296-1279	17
Usermaetre-setpenre	Ramesses II	1279-1212	67
Banenre	Merenptah	1212-1201	11
Userkheperure	Sethos II	1201-1195	6
(Menmire-setpenre	Amenmesse	1200-1196	4)
Sekhaenre/Akheperre	Siptah	1195-1189	6
Sitre-merenamun	Tawosret	1189-1187	2

Dynasty XX

Userkhaure	Sethnakhte	1187-1185	2
Usermaetre-meryamun	Ramesses III	1185-1153	32
User/Heqamaetre--setpenamun	Ramesses IV	1153-1146	7
Usermaetre-sekheperenre	Ramesses V Amenhirkopshef I	1146-1141	5
Nebmaetre-meryamun	Ramesses VI Amenhirkopshef II	1141-1133	8
Usermaetre-setpenre-meramun	Ramesses VII Itamun	1133-1125	8
Usermaetre-akhenamun	Ramesses VIII Sethhirkopshef	1125-1123	2
Neferkare-setpenre	Ramesses IX Khaemwaset I	1123-1104	19
Khepermaetre-setpenre	Ramesses X Amenhirkopshef III	1104-1094	10
Menmaetre-setpenptah	Ramesses XI Khaemwaset II	1094-1064	30

THIRD INTERMEDIATE PERIOD
Dynasty XXI

Hedjkheperre-setpenre	Smendes	1064-1038	26
Neferkare-heqawaset	Amenemnesu	1038-1034	4
(Kheperkhare-setpenamun	Pinudjem I	1049-1026	23)
Akheperre-setpenamun	Psusennes I	1034-981	53
Usermaetre-setpenamun	Amenemopet	984-974	10
Akheperre-setpenre	Osokhor	974-968	6
Netjerkheperre-meryamun	Siamun	968-948	20
(Tyetkheperure-setpenre	Psusennes II	945-940	5)

Dynasty XXII

Hedjkheperre-setpenre	Shoshenq I	948-927	21
Sekhemkheperre-setpenre	Osorkon I	927-892	35
(Heqakheperre-setpenre	Shoshenq II	895-895)	
Hedjkheprre-setpenre	Takelot I	892-877	15
Usermaetre-setpenamun	Osorkon II	877-838	39
Usermaetre-setpenre	Shoshenq III	838-798	40
Hedjkheperre-setpenre	Shoshenq IV	798-786	12
Usermaetre-setpenamun	Pimay	786-780	6
Akheperre	Shoshenq V	780-743	37

'Theban Dynasty XXIII'

Hedjkheperre-setpenamun	Harsiese	867-857	10
Hedjkheperre-setpenre	Takelot II	841-815	26
Usermaetre-setpenamun	Pedubast I	830-799	30
(?	Iuput I	815-813)	
Usermaetre-setpenamun	Osorkon III	799-769	30
Usermaetre	Takelot III	774-759	15
Usermaetre-setpenamun	Rudamun	759-739	20
-	Iny	739-734	5
Neferkare	Peftjauawybast	734-724	10

Dynasty XXIII

Sehetepibenre	Pedubast II	743-733	10
Akheperre-setpenamun	Osorkon IV	733-715	18

Dynasty XXIV

Shepsesre	Tefnakhte	731-723	8
Wahkare	Bokkhoris	723-717	6

Dynasty XXV

Seneferre	Piye	752-717	35

210

Neferkare	Shabaka	717-703	14
Djedkare	Shabataka	703-690	13
Khunefertumre	Taharqa	690-664	26
Bakare	Tanutamun	664-656	8

SAITE PERIOD
Dynasty XXVI

Wahibre	Psammetikhos I	664-610	54
Wehemibre	Nekho II	610-595	15
Neferibre	Psammetikhos II	595-589	6
Haaibre	Apries	589-570	19
Khnemibre	Amasis	570-526	44
Ankhka(en)re	Psammetikhos III	526-525	1

LATE PERIOD
Dynasty XXVII

Mesutire	Kambyses	525-522	3
Setutre	Darios I	521-486	35
?	Xerxes I	486-465	21
?	Artaxerxes I	465-424	41
?	Xerxes II	424 1	
?	Darios II	423-405	18

Dynasty XXVIII

?	Amyrtaios	404-399	5

Dynasty XXIX

Baenre-merynetjeru	Nepherites I	399-393	6
Usermaetre-setpenptah	Psamuthis	393	1
Khnemmaetre	Akhoris	393-380	13
?	Nepherites II	380	1

Dynasty XXX

Kheperkare	Nektanebo I	380-362	18
Irimaetenre	Teos	362-360	2
Senedjemibre-setpenanhur	Nektanebo II	360-342	18

Dynasty XXXI

-	Artaxerxes III Okhos	342-338	5
-	Arses	338-336	2
-	Darios III	335-332	3

HELLENISTIC PERIOD
Dynasty of Macedonia

Alexander III	332-323	9
Philippos Arrhidaeos	323-317	5
Alexander IV	317-310	7

Dynasty of Ptolemy

Ptolemy I Soter	310-282	28
Ptolemy II Philadelphos	285-246	36
Ptolemy III Euergetes I	246-222	24
Ptolemy IV Philopator	222-205	17
Ptolemy V Epiphanes	205-180	25
Ptolemy VI Philometor	180-164	16
Ptolemy VIII Euergetes II	170-163	7
Ptolemy VI (again)	163-145	18
Ptolemy VII Neos Philopator	145	1
Ptolemy VIII (again)	145-116	29
Ptolemy IX Soter II	116-110	6
Ptolemy X Alexander I	110-109	1
Ptolemy IX (again)	109-107	2
Ptolemy X (again)	107-88	19
Ptolemy IX (again)	88-80	8
(Ptolemy XI	80	1)
Ptolemy XII Neos Dionysos	80-58	22
Ptolemy XII (again)	55-51	4
Kleopatra VII Philopator	51-30	21
(Ptolemy XIII	51-57	4)
(Ptolemy XIV	47-44	3)
(Ptolemy XV Kaisaros	41-30	11)

ROMAN PERIOD	BC 30-395 AD
BYZANTINE PERIOD	395-640
ARAB PERIOD	640-1517
OTTOMAN PERIOD	1517-1805
KHEDEVAL PERIOD	1805-1914
BRITISH PROTECTORATE	1914-1922
MONARCHY	1922-1953
REPUBLIC	1953-

The Royal Cemeteries

NOTE: The following list includes all tombs used, or intended to be used, for the burials of rulers of Egypt. The necropoleis in the Nile valley holding the tombs of reigning kings are listed in approximately geographical order, from north to south. Those known only from documentary sources, and as yet undiscovered are marked with an asterisk; those which have always been known are marked '‡'. A king later reburied either at Deir el-Bahari or in the tomb of Amenophis II is marked '†'. Under 'tomb type', the following codes are used:

B	Brick tomb chambers sunk in shallow pit	SPB	Step pyramid (brick)
		TPS	True pyramid (stone)
M	Mastaba	TPB	True pyramid (brick)
R	Rock-cut tomb	T	Stone tomb chambers sunk in temple-courtyard
SPS	Step pyramid (stone)		

The suffix 'u' indicates unused for burial, either through being incomplete, or some other reason.

Site	Tomb number	Tomb type	Owner / occupant	Dynasty	Date of excavation or entry
ALEXANDRIA	-	T?	Kleopatra VII	Ptol.	*
SA EL-HAGAR (**SAIS**)	-	T	Apries	XXVI	*
	-	T	Amasis	XXVI	*
TELL EL-RUB'A (**MENDES**)	-	T	Nepherites I	XXIX	1992/3
SAN EL-HAGAR (**TANIS**)	NRT I	T	Osorkon II[1]	XXII	1939
			Takelot I	XXII	
			Shoshenq V(?)	XXII	
	NRT II	T	Pimay	XXII	1939
	NRT III	T	Psusennes I	XXI	1939/40
			Amenemopet[2]	XXI	
			Siamun(?)	XXI	

---

[1]   Probably usurped from Smendes.

[2]   Reburial?

			Psusennes II(?)	XXI	
			Shoshenq II[3]	XXII	
	NRT IV	Tu(?)	Amenemopet	XXI	1939
	NRT V	T	Shoshenq III	XXII	1945
			Shoshenq IV	XXII	
ABU ROWASH	L.I	SPB	Huni?	III	1986
	L.II	TPS	Djedefre	IV	‡
GIZA	G.I[4]	TPS	Kheops	IV	‡
	G.II	TPS	Khephren	IV	‡
	G.III	TPS	Mykerinos	IV	‡
ZAWIYET EL-ARYAN	L.XIII[5]	SPS	Nebkare	III(?)	1900
	L.XIV[6]	SPS	Horus Khaba	III	1900
ABUSIR	L.XVIII	TPS	Sahure	V	1902
	L.XX	TPS	Niuserre	V	1902
	L.XXI	TPS	Neferirkare	V	1902
	L.XXVI	M[7]	Neferefre	V	1980s
	-	TPS	Shepseskare(?)	V	-
NORTH SAQQARA	L.XXIX	TPS	Menkauhor(?)	V	1930
	L.XXX	TPS	Teti	VI	1881
	L.XXXI	TPS	Userkaf	V	1839
	L.XXXII[8]	SPS	Djoser	III	‡
	L.XXXV	TPS	Unas	V	1881
	-	SPSu	H. Sekhemkhet	III	1954
	-[9]	SPS?	?	II/III	-
	A	M	H. Hotepsekhemwy	II	1900
	B	M	H. Ninetjer	II	1938
	-	M	Sened	II	*
	-	TPS?	Merykare	X	*
SOUTH SAQQARA	L.XXXVI	TPS	Pepy I	VI	1880
	L.XXXVII	TPS	Isesi	V	1945
	L.XXXIX	TPS	Nemtyemsaf I	VI	1880
	L.XL	TPS	Ibi	VIII	1930

---

3 Reburial.

4 'The Great Pyramid'.

5 'The Unfinished Pyramid'.

6 'The Layer Pyramid'.

7 Begun as TPS.

8 'The Step Pyramid'.

9 The 'Gisr el-Modir'; traces of a similar structure seem to be visible under the sand a little way to the north.

	L.XLI	TPS	Pepy II	VI	1881
	L.XLIII[10]	M	Shepseskaf	IV	1870s
	L.XLIV	TPB	Khendjer	XIII	1929
	L.XLVI	TPBu	?	XIII	1929
DAHSHUR	L.XLIX[11]	TPS	Seneferu	IV	1839
	L.LVI[12]	TPSu	Seneferu	IV	1839
	L.XLVII	TPB	Sesostris III	XII	1894
	L.LI[13]	TPS	Ammenemes II	XII	1894
	L.LIV	TPB	Ammenemes V?	XIII	-
	L.LVIII	TPBu	Ammenemes III	XII	1894
	L.LVIII/1	R	Hor	XIII	1894
SOUTH DAHSHUR	A.	TPB	?	XIII	-
	B.	TPB	?	XIII	-
	C.	TPB	Qemau	XIII	1957
MAZGHUNA	N.	TPB	?	XIII	1911
	S.	TPB	?	XIII	1911
LISHT	L.LX	TPS	Ammenemes I	XII	1883
	L.LXI	TPS	Sesostris I	XII	1883
MEIDUM	L.LXV	TPS[14]	Huni(?)/Seneferu	III/IV	1882
HAWARA	L.LXVII	TPB	Ammenemes III	XII	1888
LAHUN	L.LXVI	TPB	Sesostris II	XII	1890
TELL EL-AMARNA	TA.26	R	Akhenaten	XVIII	1880s
	TA.27	Ru	Neferneferuaten?	XVIII	1984
	TA.28	R	Neferneferuaten?	XVIII	1984
	TA.29	Ru	Tutankhaten?	XVIII	1984
ABYDOS	B10/15/19	B	Horus Aha	I	1896
(UMM EL-QAAB)	O	B	Horus Djer	I	1896
	P	B	Seth Peribsen	II	1898
	Q	B	Horus Qaa	I	1896
	T	B	Horus Den	I	1896
	U	B	Horus Semerkhet	I	1896

---

10   'Mastabat Faraoun'.

11   'The Red Pyramid'.

12   'The Bent Pyramid'.

13   'The White Pyramid'.

14   Begun as SPS.

215

	V	B	Horus and Seth Khasekhemwy	II	1897
	X	B	Horus Adjib	I	1896
	Y	B	Meryetneith	I	1896
	Z	B	Horus Djet	I	1896
WESTERN THEBES:					
EL-TARIF	-15	R	Inyotef III	XIa	1970
	-16	R	Inyotef II	XIa	1970
	-17	R	Inyotef I	XIa	1970
DIRA ABU'L-NAGA	-	TPB	Inyotef V	XVII	*/1860s?
	-	TPB	Inyotef VI	XVII	*/1860s?
	-	TPB	Sobkemsaf I	XVII	*
	-	TPB	Kamose	XVII	*/1912?
	-	TPB	Taa I	XVII	*
	-	TPB	Taa II†	XVII	*
	-	R?	Amenophis I†	XVIII	*?
DEIR EL-BAHARI	DBXI.14	R	Montjuhotpe II	XIb	1903
MEDINET HABU	MH.1	T	Harsiese	Th.XXIII	1928
	-	T?	Osorkon III	Th.XXIII	*
BIBAN EL-MOLUK	KV.1	R	Ramesses VII	XX	‡
(V. OF KINGS)	KV.2	R	Ramesses IV†	XX	‡
	KV.4	R	Ramesses XI	XX	‡
	KV.6	R	Ramesses IX†	XX	‡
	KV.7	R	Ramesses II†	XIX	‡
	KV.8	R	Merenptah†	XIX	‡
	KV.9	R	Ramesses V†/VI†	XX	‡
	KV.10	R	Amenmesse	XIX	‡
	KV.11	R	Ramesses III†18	XX	‡
	KV.14	R	Tawosret/ Sethnakhte	XIX XX	‡
	KV.15	R	Sethos II†	XIX	‡
	KV.16	R	Ramesses I†	XIX	1817
	KV.17	R	Sethos II†	XIX	1817
	KV.18	R	Ramesses X	XX	‡
	KV.20	R	Tuthmosis I/ Hatshepsut	XVIII	1903
	WV.22	R	Amenophis III†	XVIII	1799

---

15 'Saffel-Bagar'.

16 'Saffel-Qisasiya'.

17 'SaffDawaba'.

18 Begun for Sethnakhte.

	WV.23	R	Ay	XVIII	1816
	WV.25	Ru	Amenophis IV/		
			Neferneferuaten?	XVIII	1816
	VK.34	R	Tuthmosis III†	XVIII	1898
	VK.35	R	Amenophis II	XVIII	1898
	VK.38	R	Tuthmosis I[19]	XVIII	1898
	VK.42	R	Tuthmosis II†	XVIII	1900
	VK.43	R	Tuthmosis IV†	XVIII	1903
	VK.47	R	Siptah†	XIX	1905
	VK.55	R	Neferneferuaten[20]	XVIII	1907
	VK.57	R	Horemheb	XVIII	1908
	VK.62	R	Tutankhamun	XVIII	1922
EL-KURRU	Ku.15	TPS	Shabaka	XXV	1919
	Ku.16	TPS	Tanutamun	XXV	1919
	Ku.17	TPS	Piye	XXV	1919
	Ku.18	TPS	Shabataka	XXV	1919
NURI	Nu.1	TPS	Taharqa	XXV	1916

---

[19] Constructed for reburial by Tuthmosis III.

[20] Reburial.

217

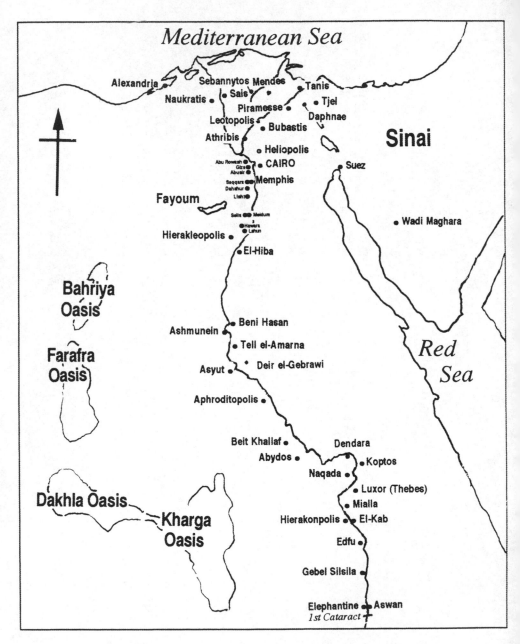

Fig. 69. Map of Egypt.

218

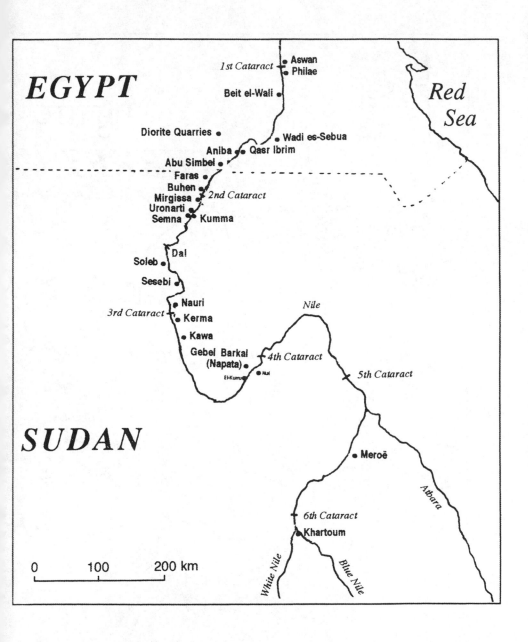

EGYPT

Red
Sea

1st Cataract ● Aswan
● Philae

Beit el-Wali ●

Diorite Quarries ●

● Wadi es-Sebua

Aniba ● ● Qasr Ibrim

Abu Simbel ●

Faras ●
Buhen ●
Mirgissa ● 2nd Cataract
Uronarti ●
Semna ●● Kumma

Dal

Soleb ●
Sesebi ●

● Nauri
3rd Cataract ● Kerma
● Kawa

Gebel Barkal
(Napata) ● 4th Cataract
El-Kurru ● ● Nuri
5th Cataract

Nile

SUDAN

● Meroë

Abara

6th Cataract
● Khartoum

0   100   200 km

White Nile

Blue Nile

Fig. 70. Map of Nubia.

219

Fig. 71. Map of the Near East in the New Kingdom.

MPIRE

arch-
nish

MITANNI

Nineveh

Aleppo

Tigris

Ashur

YRIA

Euphrates

ASSYRIA

desh

IRÂQ

mascus

Baghdad

Babylon

BABYLONIA

Ur

SUMER

DAN

0   500 km

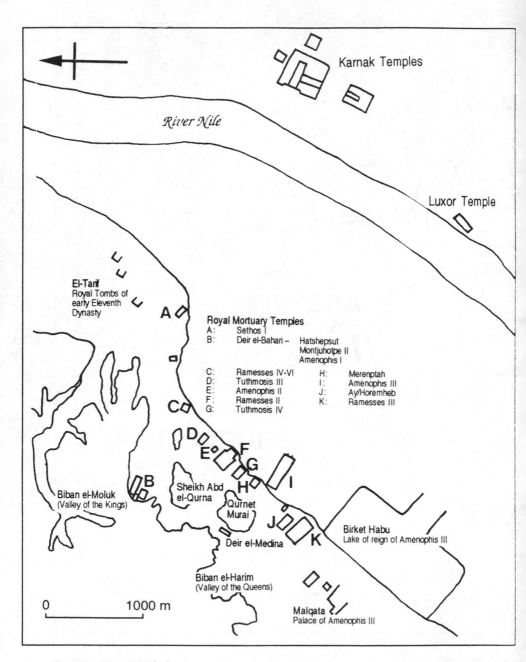

Fig. 72. Map of Thebes.

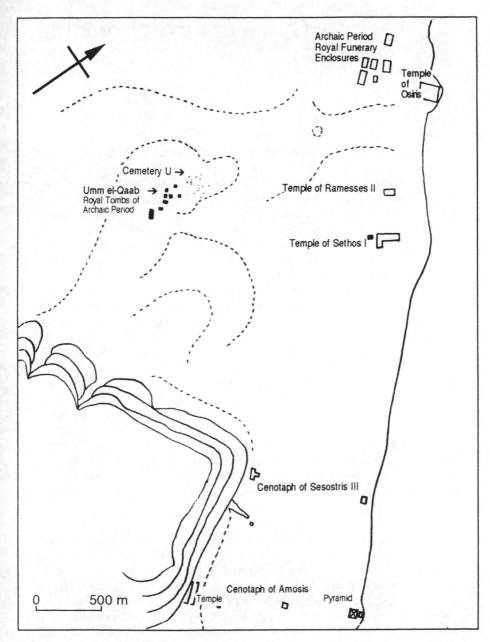

Fig. 73. Map of Abydos.

223

Guide to further reading

The literature on ancient Egypt is manifold – and of distinctly mixed quality. In particular, most 'popular' works lag a long way behind current research, and often state as 'fact' theories which have been discredited since the 1960s, or even earlier. There are also reprints of very old works that are of only antiquarian interest –- although dressed up in smart new covers giving little indication of their vintage. That is not to say that all modern scholarly books and articles are significantly better! The international nature of the subject also means that many fundamental works are only available in non-English languages and/or difficult-to-find periodicals.

For more or less exhaustive digests of information there are two modern encyclopedias, K.A. Bard (ed.), *Encyclopedia of the Archaeology of Ancient Egypt* (London: Routledge, 1999), in one volume, and D.B. Redford (ed.), *Oxford Encyclopedia of Ancient Egypt* (OUP, 2000) in three. Much more concise is I. Shaw and P. Nicholson, *British Museum Dictionary of Ancient Egypt* (British Museum Press, 1995). Amongst the vast number of 'coffee table' books on ancient Egypt, by far the best is R. Schulz and M. Seidel (eds.), *Egypt: World of the Pharaohs* (Cologne: Könemann, 1998).

The guide below focuses almost exclusively on book-length publications in English which cover Egyptian *history*, and should be orderable from public libraries. Most contain bibliographies which will allow the interested person to follow-up the more specialist literature.

General
There is a dearth of good, up-to-date general histories of Egypt. By far the best is B.G. Trigger, B.J. Kemp, D. O'Connor and A.B. Lloyd, *Ancient Egypt: a Social History* (Cambridge University Press, 1983), although now beginning to show its age. For the overall political, as against social, picture, Bill Manley's *Penguin Historical Atlas of Ancient Egypt* (London: Penguin Books, 1996) is excellent. For more detail, one has resort to a number of works, all of which are more or less badly out of date, although in one case published only recently:

224

The Cambridge Ancient History, Third Edition (Cambridge University Press, 1971ff).

A.H. Gardiner, *Egypt of the Pharaohs* (Oxford University Press, 1961).

N.-C. Grimal, *A History of Ancient Egypt* (Oxford: Blackwell, 1992).

W.C. Hayes, *The Scepter of Egypt,* 2vv (1953-9, reprinted New York: Abrams, 1990).

A basic compilation of information on individual pharaohs is also provided by P.A. Clayton, *Chronicle of the Pharaohs* (London: Thames & Hudson, 1994).

There are a number of digests that include the most important historical texts; J.H. Breasted, *Ancient Records of Egypt,* 5vv (1905, reprinted London: Histories and Mysteries of Man, 1988) is outdated, but the only generally-available comprehensive source. A selection are, however, included in M. Lichtheim, *Ancient Egyptian Literature,* 3vv (University of California Press, 1975-80), and W.K. Simpson (ed.), *The Literature of Ancient Egypt* (Yale University Press, 1973).

A view of developments in Egyptological thinking, aimed at the non-specialist, is available in the quarterly magazine *KMT: a Modern Journal of Egyptology* (*KMT* Communications, San Francisco). There is also *Egyptian Archaeology,* published by London's Egypt Exploration Society, which covers the most recent events in the subject. The same organization also publishes the much 'heavier' *Journal of Egyptian Archaeology.* In the United States of America, the latter's approximate equivalent is the *Journal of the American Research Center in Egypt,* based in New York and Cairo.

Frequent mentions are made in the text to the burial-places of the kings of Egypt. The basic sources for the pyramids of the Old and Middle Kingdoms (and the Twenty-fifth Dynasty) are given under Chapters IV and V, while New Kingdom and later sepulchres are covered in, amongst others, A.M. Dodson, *After the Pyramids* (London: Rubicon, 2000), E. Hornung, *The Valley of the Kings: Horizon of Eternity* (New York: Timken, 1990) and C.N. Reeves and R.H. Wilkinson, *Complete Valley of the Kings* (London: Thames & Hudson, 1996).

For basic information on the archaeological sites of Egypt, one cannot better J. Baines and J. Malek, *Atlas of Ancient Egypt* (Oxford: Phaidon/Facts on File, 1980), together with the encyclopedias mentioned above.

Chapters I and II

The geography, culture and 'daily life' of ancient Egypt have been covered by many books. Probably the best generally available book on life in the Nile valley in Pharaonic times is T.G..H. James' *Pharaoh's People* (London: Bodley Head/Oxford: OUP, 1984), but Barbara Merz' *Red Land, Black Land* (New York: Dell, 1966) is both informative and highly entertaining. On pharaonic titulary and related matters, see Stephen Quirke, *Who were the Pharaohs?* (British Museum Press, 1990).

Going into more detail, for an analysis of what made ancient Egypt 'tick', one cannot do better than read Barry J. Kemp, *Ancient Egypt: Anatomy of A Civilization* (London: Routledge, 1989). Aspects of agriculture, irrigation and such-like are covered by Karl W. Butzer, *Early Hydraulic Civilization in Egypt: a Study in Cultural Ecology* (University of Chicago Press, 1976).

Two of the best works on Egyptian religion are S. Quirke, *Ancient Egyptian Religion* (British Museum Press, 1992), and E. Hornung, *Conceptions of God in Ancient Egypt* (London: Routledge and Kegan Paul, 1983), the latter being a real attempt to understand the true meaning of some of the Egyptians' beliefs.

Chapter III

The earliest years of Egypt are covered by B. Midant-Reynes, *The Prehistory of Egypt* (Oxford: Blackwell, 2000), M.A. Hoffman, *Egypt Before the Pharaohs* (London: Routledge and Kegan Paul, 1979), A.J. Spencer, *Early Egypt: the Rise of Civilisation in the Nile Valley* (British Museum Publications, 1993) and T.A.H. Wilkinson, *Early Dynastic Egypt* (London: Routledge, 1999).

Chapters IV and V

The era of the pyramid-builders is usually approached from the point of view of their funerary monuments – inevitably, given the paucity of other sources of information. The basic works are:

I.E.S. Edwards, *The Pyramids of Egypt,* 3rd Edition (London: Penguin, 1985).

A. Fakhry, *The Pyramids,* 2nd Edition (University of Chicago Press, 1969).

M. Lehner, *The Complete Pyramids* (London: Thames & Hudson, 1997).

A very well-illustrated book covering the pyramids and kings of the Fifth Dynasty is M. Verner's *Forgotten Pharaohs, Lost Pyramids: Abusir* (Prague: Acadamia–Skodaexport, 1994). The material culture of the time as a whole is covered by the exhibition catalogue, *Egyptian Art in the Age of the Pyramids* (New York: Abrams, 1999), with J. Malek and W. Forman's *In the Shadow of the Pyramids* (Cairo: AUC Press, 1986) a good general work The nobility and bureaucracy of the Old

Kingdom are covered by N. Strudwick, *The Administration of the Old Kingdom* (London: Kegan Paul International, 1985).

Chapters VI and VII
The First Intermediate Period and the Middle Kingdom are badly served by readily accessible literature. The relevant chapters in the works cited General section, above, are useful, as are the exhibition catalogues, J.D. Bourriau, *Pharaohs and Mortals: Egyptian Art in the Middle Kingdom* (Cambridge University Press, 1988), and Gay Robins (ed.), *Beyond the Pyramids: Egyptian Regional Art from the Museo Egizio, Turin* (Atlanta: Emory University Museum, 1991). A collection of papers covering certain aspects of the period is to be found in S. Quirke (ed.), *Middle Kingdom Studies* (Sia Publications, 1991), with foreign connections of the First Intermediate Period covered by William A. Ward, *Egypt and the East Mediterranean World 2200-1900 BC* (American University in Beirut, 1971). H.E. Winlock's *Rise and Fall of the Middle Kingdom at Thebes* (New York: Macmillan, 1947) remains good for the first part of the period, but badly flawed and out of date for the second. Absolutely fundamental for the Thirteenth Dynasty and the following period is K. Ryholt's *The Political Situation in Egypt during the Second Intermediate Period* (Copenhagen: Museum Tusculanum Press, 1997).

Chapter VIII
The background to, and aftermath of, the wars against the Hyksos are best given (with differing interpretations) by Ryholt, just above, and D.B. Redford, *Egypt, Canaan and Israel in Ancient Times* (Princeton University Press, 1992). The Kamose stela is published by L. Habachi, *Second stela of Kamose and his struggle against the Hyksos* (Glückstadt, 1972), while Amosis' campaigns are covered by Cl. Vandersleyen, *Les guerres d'Amosis* (Brussels: Fondation Égyptologique Reine Élisabeth, 1971). The material culture of the period is well-covered in the work by Hayes, cited in the General section.

Chapter IX
Tuthmosis III and Hatshepsut's period of joint reign, and the various problems associated with it are fully covered by P.F. Dorman, *The Monuments of Senenmut* (London: Kegan Paul International, 1988). The wars of Tuthmosis III are covered by many of the general works.

Chapter X
The Amarna is replete with problems, and almost every writer has

produced different conclusions concerning each of them. Key areas of dispute are whether or not Amenophis III and Akhenaten ruled together, and the identity and dating of the reign(s) of Smenkhka-re/Neferneferuaten, to name but two. Unfortunately, much of the still-live argumentation is in learned journals, difficult of access to the general reader. However, the following books give a glimpse at the various scholarly perspectives:

The reign of Amenophis III is best approached via the exhibition catalogue, A.P. Kozloff and B.M. Bryan, *Egypt's Dazzling Sun: Amen-hotep III and his World* (Indiana University Press, 1992). Two views of Akhenaten's reign, pro- and anti-coregency, are given by C. Aldred, *Akhenaten, King of Egypt* (London: Thames & Hudson, 1988), and D.B. Redford, *Akhenaten, the Heretic King* (Princeton University Press, 1984). Some of the more recent developments may be traced in the semi-popular occasional publication *Amarna Letters* (*KMT* Communic-ations, 1991ff), and in the exhibition catalogue, Freed, R., et al. (eds.), *Pharaohs of the Sun: Akhenaten, Nefertiti and Tutankhamen* (Boston: Museum of Fine Arts, 1999)

For many years, the easiest-accessible work on Tutankhamun has been the much-reprinted C. Desroches-Noblecourt, *Tutankhamen*; this is, however, now sadly dated, and awaits replacement. The king's tomb and his reign are summarised by Nicholas Reeves' *Complete Tutankhamun* (London: Thames & Hudson, 1990). The early life of Horemheb is covered in G.T. Martin, *The Hidden Tombs of Memphis* (Thames & Hudson, 1991); his reign and that of Ay are covered in a general way by Aldred, and by Kitchen in the book cited for the next chapter.

• Chapters XI and XII

Fundamental for the Nineteenth Dynasty is K.A. Kitchen, *Pharaoh Triumphant* (Aris and Phillips, 1982). Useful for the background to Ramesses II's wars is W.J. Murnane, *The Road to Kadesh*, Second Edition (University of Chicago Press, 1990).

The troubles surrounding the end of the Nineteenth Dynasty are not really covered outside the specialist journals. Something of the background is, however, covered in *Pharaoh Triumphant*.

Chapters XIII, XIV and XV

Ramesses III has largely to be investigated via the various General historical books, but his later years are well-covered by the book by A.J. Peden cited just below. The king's opponents, the Sea Peoples, are, however, covered by N.K. Sandars, *The Sea Peoples: Warriors of the Mediterranean* (London: Thames & Hudson, 1985).

Ramesses IV is the only king thus far to have an English-language monograph dedicated to him: A.J. Peden, *The Reign of Ramesses IV* (Warminster: Aris & Phillips, 1994). For the later Ramessides and all kings of the Third Intermediate Period, the exhaustive study is K.A. Kitchen, *The Third Intermediate Period in Egypt*, Second Edition (Warminster: Aris and Phillips, 1986). Many modifications to the basic structure presented now need to be made; for some, see A. Leahy (ed.), *Libya and Egypt, c1300-750 BC* (London: SOAS, 1990), and the summ-ary in my article in *KMT* 6:2 (1995).

Radical reassessment of the whole period, with many kings and dynasties overlapped to reduce dates by centuries is published by P. James, *Centuries of Darkness* (London: Jonathan Cape, 1991), and D. Rohl, *A Test of Time* (London: Channel 4, 1995). In spite of some persuasive points, the whole approach is extreme, and in many key areas, particularly in the Twenty-first Dynasty, simply cannot be squared with the evidence of certain categories of funerary material.

Chapter XVI
The Nubian kings and their origins are dealt with by R. Morkot, *The Black Pharaohs* (London: Rubicon, 2000), with a number of new inter-pretations. They are also extensively discussed by Kitchen. A large-scale work on the whole of of Nubian history is W.Y. Adams, *Nubia: Corridor to Africa* (London: Allen Lane, 1984).

Chapters XVII and XVIII
The last native rulers of Egypt, and the interposing Persian rulers, are covered in English by Alan Lloyd's chapter of *Ancient Egypt: a Social History*, his *Herodotus Book II, Commentary 1-98* (Leiden: Brill, 1976) and by current and forthcoming sections of the *Cambridge Ancient History*. The basic source remains, however, F.K. Kienitz, *Die politische Geschichte Ägyptens vom 7. bis zum 4. Jahrhundert vor der Zeitwende* (Berlin, 1953).

Epilogue
The later history of ancient Egypt is part of that of the Classical world, and may be traced from that direction in many works, in particular the *Cambridge Ancient History*. A good bibliography is included in the Alan K. Bowman's cultural survey, *Egypt after the Pharaohs* (British Museum Publications, 1986).

Byzantine (Coptic) and later Egypt are covered by a vast range of publications, but consideration is beyond the scope of this book.

Index

Egyptian rulers are small-capitalised.

Abbreviations:

GWA -	God's Wife of Amun
HPA -	High Priest of Amun at Thebes
HPM -	High Priest of Ptah at Memphis
HPH -	High Priest of Re at Heliopolis
LE -	Lower Egyptian
UE -	Upper Egyptian

Pramesse (General; later RAMESSES I), 118-119.
Pramessu (LE vizier), 130.
Prehirwenemef A (son of RAMESSES II), 126.
priest, 4, 6, 8, 35, 37, 89, 92-93, 115, 130, 135,
    137, 146, 148, 150-151, 153-156, 159,
    161-162, 164-165, 167-168, 170-173, 184,
    188, 191, 230.
Psametjik (son of AMASIS, later
    PSAMMETIKHOS III), 194.
Psametjik (son of NEKHO I; later
    PSAMMETIKHOS I), 186-187.
PSAMMETIKHOS I, 187-188, 190, 210.
PSAMMETIKHOS II, 191, 210.
PSAMMETIKHOS III, 194-195, 210.
PSAMUTHIS, 211.
PSUSENNES I, 63, 154, 156-157, 159. 209, 213.
PSUSENNES II, 161, 209, 213.
Ptah, 3, 23, 37, 89, 92, 110, 115, 126-127,
    130-131, 146, 167-168, 170, 179, 188.
Ptah (division of army), 126.
Ptahemakhet i (HPM), 131.
Ptahemhat-Ty (HPM), 115.
Ptahmose (HPA), 91.
Ptahshepses (son of PEPY II?), 43.
Ptahudjankhef (Governor of Herakleopolis),
    171.
PTOLEMY I, 202, 211.
PTOLEMY II-IV, 211.
PTOLEMY V, 23, 211.
PTOLEMY VI-XV, 211.
Pudukhepa (Queen of the Hittites), 128.
Punt, 36, 41-42, 80, 82,116, 145.

Qadesh, 84, 86-87, 121, 126-127, 131.
Qarqar, Battle of, 167.

Rahotpe (HPM), 131.
Rahotpe (son of SENEFERU), 29.
Raia (father-in-law of SETHOS I), 122.
Ramesse (son of SETHOS I, later RAMESSES II),
    123.
Ramesse A (son of RAMESSES II), 129.
Ramesse C (son of RAMESSES III; later king as
    RAMESSES IV), 146 .
Ramesse D (son of RAMESSES VII), 150.
Ramesse-Ankhefenmut (son of PSUSENNES I),
    157, 158.
Ramesse-khaemnetjeru: see Bay.
Ramessenakhte (HPA), 150.
RAMESSES I, 118, 208, 216.
RAMESSES II, 91, 123, 126-127. 131, 147-149,
    208, 216.
RAMESSES III, 143, 145, 150, 159, 209, 216

RAMESSES IV, 146, 148-149, 209, 216.
RAMESSES V, 149, 209, 216.
RAMESSES VI, 149, 209, 216.
RAMESSES VII, 150, 209, 216.
RAMESSES VIII, 150, 209.
RAMESSES IX, 150, 209, 216.
RAMESSES X, 151, 209, 216.
RAMESSES XI, 151, 153, 209, 216.
RAMESSES-PSUSENNES: see PSUSENNES I.
RAMESSES-SIPTAH: SEE SIPTAH.
Ramesseum, 131.
Ramose (son[?] of AMOSIS), 76.
Ramose (UE Vizier), 91.
Re, 3, 8-9, 35, 37, 40. 44, 49, 51-52, 61, 69,
    79-80, 83-84, 91, 95-96, 101, 103-104,
    110, 116-117. 129-130, 143, 145-146.
    149, 155-156, 165, 168, 179, 190, 203,
    210-211, 230.
Re (division of army), 126
Red Sea, 16, 36, 42, 55, 80.
Reddjedet (alleged mother of USERKAF,
    SAHURE and NEFERIRKARE), 35.
Rehoboam (King of Judah), 162.
Rekhmire (UE Vizier), 87.
Reuser (husband of Reddjedet), 35.
Rewer (Vizier), 39.
Roma-Roy (HPA), 130, 135, 137.
RUDAMUN, 172-173, 177, 210.
Ruia (mother-in-law of SETHOS I),122.

Sabni (of Aswan), 41.
SAHURE, 34-37, 80, 205, 214.
Saqqara, 14-18, 20-21, 24, 26, 33-34. 38. 40,
    42, 44, 46, 67, 70, 110-111, 114-119,
    167, 170, 184, 190, 194, 214.
'SCORPION', 12, 15.
Scythians. 64.
Sea Peoples, 144. 148, 228.
Sehel, 23.
Seila, 27.
Sekhemkare (son of KHEPHREN; Vizier). 32.
    37.
Semna, 61-62, 79, 175.
SENEFERU, 3, 26-30, 56, 62, 205, 215.
Senenmut, 81, 84, 227.
Sennacherib (King of Assyria), 182.
Senwosret (father of AMMENEMES I), 56.
SESOSTRIS I, 57-58, 206, 215.
SESOSTRIS II, 59, 206, 215.
SESOSTRIS III, 58-64, 94, 206, 215.
Seth, 6. 18-21, 142.
Seth (division of army), 126.
SETH PERBISEN, 19

SETHHIRKOPSHEF: see RAMESSES VIII.
Sethhirkopshef A (son of RAMESSES II), 129.
Sethhirkopshef C (son of RAMESSES III; later
    king as RAMESSES VIII), 146.
SETHNAKHTE, 139, 141-142, 209, 216.
SETHOS I, 44, 119, 121, 123-125, 208.
SETHOS II, 139.
Sethy (father of RAMESSES I), 119.
Sethy (LE Vizier), 130.
Sethy (son of RAMESSES I; later SETHOS I), 119.
Sethy-Merenptah A (son of MERENPTAH, later
    SETHOS II), 133.
Sethy-Merenptah B (son of SETHOS II), 135, 139
SHABAKA, 182, 184-185, 188, 210.
SHABATAKA, 182, 210, 217.
Shalmaneser III (King of Assyria), 167.
Sharuhen, 75.
Shedsunefertum A (HPM), 162.
Shemay (of Koptos), 45.
Shepenwepet I (GWA; daughter of OSORKON III),
    172-174.
Shepenwepet II (GWA; daughter of PIYE), 188.
SHEPSESKAF, 32-34, 37, 205, 215.
SHEPSESKARE, 38, 205, 214.
SHESHI, 207.
SHOSHENQ A (CHIEF OF THE MA; GRANDFATHER OF
    SHOSHENQ I), 159.
Shoshenq B (Chief of the Ma; later King
    SHOSHENQ I), 161.
Shoshenq C (HPA, later King SHOSHENQ II, 164.
Shoshenq D (HPM; son of OSORKON II), 165, 167-
    168.
SHOSHENQ I, 159-165, 182, 209.
SHOSHENQ II, 164, 209, 214.
SHOSHENQ III, 168-169, 209, 214.
SHOSHENQ IV, 168, 209, 214.
SHOSHENQ V, 174, 209, 214.
Shuppiliumash (King of the Hittites), 113.
SIAMUN, 159, 161-162, 166, 209, 213.
Siamun (son of AMOSIS), 76.
Sinuhe, Story of, 58.
SIPTAH, 39, 139-141, 209, 216.
Sitamun A (daughter of AMOSIS), 76.
Sitamun B (daughter-wife of AMENOPHIS III), 95,
    129.
Sitiah (wife of TUTHMOSIS III), 88.
Sitre (wife of RAMESSES I), 119.
SMENDES, 153-155, 164, 209.
Smendes II (General; HPA), 157, 159.
Smendes III (HPA, son of Osorkon I), 164.
SMENKHKARE, 96, 104-106, 207-208, 227.
SOBKEMSAF I, 208.
SOBKEMSAF II, 208.

SOBKHOTPE III, 69, 207.
SOBKHOTPE IV, 69-70.
Sobkkhu, 60.
SOBKNEFERU, 67, 105, 206.
Soleb, 91.
Solomon (King of Israel), 162.
Somtutefnakhte (Shipmaster), 188.
Sparta, 199.
Sudan, 1, 4, 9, 36, 79, 91, 175, 181, 184.
Syria-Palestine, 15, 76-77, 86, 88, 101, 109,
    113, 120, 126, 128, 143-144, 182, 184,
    191, 200.

TAA I, 208, 216.
TAA II 71-73, 216.
TAHARQA, 37, 182-186, 210, 217.
Takelot B (HPM), 167-168.
Takelot E (HPA), 172.
Takelot F (HPA; possibly later King
    TAKELOT II?), 165, 170.
Takelot G (HPA; later king as TAKELOT III),
    172.
TAKELOT I, 164, 209, 213.
TAKELOT II, 169, 171, 210.
TAKELOT III, 174, 210.
Takhat (wife of SETHOS II), 133, 136.
Takheredeneset (mother of AMASIS), 194.
TANUTAMUN, 186-188, 210, 217.
TAWOSRET, 139, 141-142, 209, 216.
Tefibi (Nomarch of Asyut), 46.
TEFNAKHTE, 177-178, 180-181, 186-187, 210.
Tem (wife of MONTJUHOTPE II), 53.
Tentamenopet (wife of SHOSHENQ III), 168.
Tentamun (wife of SMENDES), 153.
Tentheta (wife of AMASIS), 194.
Tentsai (wife of OSORKON III), 172.
TEOS, 200, 211.
TETI, 38, 40, 205, 214.
Teti-en (rebel), 75.
Tetisherit (mother of TAA II), 72.
Thebes, 3, 45-47, 49, 53, 55, 57, 71-72, 87,
    90-91, 94, 96, 99, 107, 110, 112,
    124-125, 131, 135, 140, 145, 148, 151,
    153-156, 161, 164-165, 167-169,
    171-173, 176-178, 181, 183, 186-189,
Thebes (cont.), 192, 194, 216, 222, 227, 230.
Thracians, 64.
Thutmose B (HPM; son of AMENOPHIS III),
    92, 117, 123, 130.
Tia (brother-in-law of RAMESSES II), 123.
Tiye (wife of AMENOPHIS III), 89, 91, 93-95,
    97, 106, 110, 113, 146.
Tiye (wife of RAMESSES III), 146.